A Composers Eleven

NEVILLE CARDUS

A Composers Eleven

With drawings by
MILEIN COSMAN

LONDON

Jonathan Cape
THIRTY BEDFORD SQUARE

'TEN COMPOSERS' FIRST PUBLISHED 1945
SECOND IMPRESSION 1946
THIRD IMPRESSION 1948
FOURTH IMPRESSION 1952

★

'A COMPOSERS ELEVEN' FIRST PUBLISHED 1958

PRINTED IN GREAT BRITAIN
IN THE CITY OF OXFORD
AT THE ALDEN PRESS
BOUND BY A. W. BAIN & CO. LTD.,
LONDON

Contents

PREFACE 7

I FRANZ SCHUBERT 1797-1828 13

II WAGNER 1813-1883 31

III BRAHMS 1833-1897 65

IV ANTON BRUCKNER 1824-1896 89

V GUSTAV MAHLER 1860-1911 105

VI STRAUSS, THE TRAGIC-COMEDIAN
1864-1949 129

VII CÉSAR FRANCK 1822-1890 159

VIII DEBUSSY 1862-1918 171

IX EDWARD ELGAR 1857-1934 193

X DELIUS 1863-1934 215

XI SIBELIUS 1865-1957 239

Preface

THE call for a fifth edition of this book seems to place me under an obligation, for courtesy's sake, to perform something more than the usual bow of acknowledgment; the least I can do to express my gratitude (and surprise) is to give an encore. I have therefore revised *Ten Composers* thoroughly, adding considerably to the chapters on Mahler, Strauss, Delius and Debussy; also I have contributed a new chapter on Bruckner, thus making a Composers XI. Those of my readers who are interested in cricket may amuse themselves by naming the batting order and the sorts of bowling which would most likely suit the members of this immortal team and company: Mahler fast and erratic, with a puzzling slow ball; Debussy cunning flight and possibly in control of a googly; Sibelius good length and steady with the new ball?

The subjects of each chapter were not chosen entirely at random; they are related to a background of music stretching from the beginning of the nineteenth century to Sibelius, who lived long enough to see himself grouped amongst the reactionaries against romantic expression. I have included Bruckner in the sequence because he goes naturally into the genealogy, and because he is not yet understood in this country. I need not direct the attention of the reader to certain omissions. If Brahms, why not Schumann? Where are Berlioz and Liszt? But I have not aspired to comprehensive history, or tried to negotiate every ebb and flow of style. I have not thought of presenting

the nineteenth-century composers in the round; I have
been mainly interested in the soil, the roots, the habitat.
Schumann I love; but I see him as one fine fruit amongst
others, not a seed. The importance of Liszt as a representative figure and influence is beyond argument; as a maker of
music he frankly does not set my pen moving. Berlioz
eluded me, in spite of several attempts to see him steadily
and in the whole with eyes of admiration. He loomed large
until I began to write; then he ran to bone.

I have been at some trouble to observe the truth that
genius and metier and the cultural environment are almost
indivisible in any creative process; at the same time I have
tried to convey a sense of a composer's own power. I suppose
that nowadays I should in politeness confess to one and all
that I do not share the contemporary attitude to music-
criticism and to music. A great composition to me is –
speaking naively no doubt – an incarnation of a genius, all
that was ever of him of consequence. The body and brain
of Beethoven, as so much physiology or the theme thereof,
have rotted away long since; what we hear in the concert
hall is not only a symphony, not a thing-in-itself, not just
an important link in a chain of music's evolution. It is
Beethoven's mind, spirit and (as important) his juice and his
humours. We should make a kind of Eucharist of our
listening. I do not understand the current method of
criticism which affects to detach itself from a work of music
and regard it more or less as an analytical chemist regards
the contents of his test tube, or as Mr Micawber regarded,
not severely, the nail in the wall. I am as impatient as the
next 'objective' critic of the vice of writing around music.
But I have no time for technical analysis that is not directed
to its findings by some imaginative insight. It is a hard job
to discuss in words the reason why notes and forms of music
are significant, and of what they are significant in terms of

human emotion and experience. Still, as Pooh Bah says, a man might try. If music is not a language in which the Beethovens and Mozarts and Sibeliuses speak and give account of themselves exactly as the Shakespeares, Goethes, Rilkes and Eliots speak and give account of themselves in words, then I and many others have been wasting our time on it. If music were for me only a matter of the arrangement of patterns and designs in tones it would not hold my attention half as arrestingly as it is held any winter morning by the marvellous tracery of frost on the lawn or window-pane. It is necessary that the writer of music should keep his ear on the notes; it is as necessary that he should have the gift of hearing them all in a context that is related to a grasp of a particular style. Adagio in Bruckner is vastly different from adagio in Mahler; crescendo in Schubert sweeps us into a world never entered by Rossini. Why these differences of forms and motions? It should be the aim of the writer on music to explain or illumine the musical traits that make the style that is the man himself related to his environment.

London,
March 1958

I

Franz Schubert
1797–1828

Franz Schubert

A WEEK or two before he died Schubert called on Sechter, the court organist of Vienna, and proposed to take lessons from him in fugal writing. There is reason for supposing that Schubert was not so much concerned about his equipment for composition as about his chances of getting a job as second court organist; a little show of erudition would no doubt strengthen his claims. The savants, professors and general alumni have found in this Schubert–Sechter episode certain proof that Schubert anticipated their own view of him as a composer inspired but ill-equipped technically, commanding scant counterpoint. Criticism has a brisk way of pointing out where genius could have been improved. But it is a comforting thought, which reflection will stimulate, that on the whole the geniuses somehow absorb the amount of culture they need, and discover the adequate technique of expression. Counterpoint in any excess or severity would have been as much a hindrance in Schubert as lack of it in Bach. A Schubert who weighed every note would not have been the Schubert we know; he would have been a different Schubert. And imagination simply cannot conceive a different Schubert, even if reason, working abstractedly, can.

Not only the dons have detected absence of fundamental brainwork from Schubert's music. Bernard Shaw, when he contemplated the C major Symphony during his sparetime activities as a music critic, wrote these memorable sentences:

'Much as I appreciate the doughtiness with which Sir
George Grove fought Schubert's battle in England, yet now
it is won I instinctively bear back a little, feeling that before
any artist, whatever his branch may be, can take his place
with the highest, there is a certain price to be paid in
headwork, and that Schubert never paid that price.'[1] With
immense knowledge and forensic argumentation Donald
Tovey tried to demonstrate Schubert's mastery of form; but
I do not think that he made enough of the fact that every
genius requires to master only a certain kind and amount
of form, and only as much erudition as will cultivate his
particular garden. Schubert no doubt rushed in at times
where only fools are not afraid to tread. As Gilbert Chester-
ton once remarked, the Greenhorn is taken in, and the
All-too-knowing ones are cast out. The risks embraced by
Schubert in the finale of the C major Symphony, for
example, were terrible; he trembles bar by bar on the thin
edge that separates the ridiculous from the sublime. From
the rum-ti-tum of a Marche Militaire, worked up to a
Rossini crescendo, he builds a giant's causeway leading to
heaven knows where; reiterated blows come from the
foundry of the sublime. The C major Symphony was
Schubert's tour de force; he, who is supposed to have run
too fast to read, made hundreds of erasures in the first score
of the work, scratched out with a penknife. We are free to
assume that he could not cope symphonically with the
profusion of ideas that was overwhelming him; for they
were essentially lyrical ideas. And here we come to the main
line of approach to Schubert; you can easily be lured down
an entangled bypath, luxuriant but misleading. Each genius
may be estimated only by the laws set up by the peculiar
nature or order of his art; each genius is open to criticism
only when he forgets those laws. All the counterpoint in

[1] *Music in London, 1890-94*, p. 53.

the world could not have changed Schubert to a symphonist of far-reaching and binding logic.

For he was the first vagrant composer, and he emerged from circumstances which have not been known before or since the advent of Schubert in the history of the development of music. The art had for centuries worshipped in turn God and the Sublime; it was the heavenly art, a mystery of numbers. In course of time it became as much a science as an art, with the Netherlanders spinning their notes, mathematics of tone staggering the mind. Then from church and cloister and pedant's study music entered the *salon* and drawing-room of civilized men and women; the composer donned his livery but none the less he had to know his technique equally with the cook and the perruquier. Mozart, though inspired of heaven, composed in the polite manner of his day; he added genius to culture and established style. Beethoven shook the ordered palace of the eighteenth-century symphony to its foundations, no doubt; the wind of his revolution made havoc on the lawns of a Versailles of music. But he was a master musician and with his vision and ethic he remained aloof from the changed scene. For the period of Biedermeier was at hand; the multitudinous world of the Napoleonic adventure had narrowed in Vienna to a round well of cosiness when Schubert came to full song. The petite bourgeoisie and their more comfortable Stimmung prepared a new soil and atmosphere for the arts, most of all in Vienna. If we consider Schubert in relation to his musical background during the years extending from 1797 to 1828 we can think of him as one who strayed when very young into Mozart's groomed garden and picked a bloom or two, then went along the slopes of the height tossed up by Beethoven's earthquake, and near the summit found wildflowers in plenty. It is a wonder he was not arrested by the custodians of Mount

Parnassus for loitering without visible means of support – in other words, without counterpoint. He was unmistakably the first vagrant composer.

II

Mozart was music; Schubert was song. A difference of kind. So pure was the impulse to lyric warmth and inflexion in Schubert that his instrumental works are full of themes that ask to be given the spontaneity and quick transitions of song prompted by poetic words or ideas. Schubert seldom wrote themes that are instrumental in the way themes of Mozart are instrumental. Melody in Mozart is seldom at the mercy of unexpected poetic impulse. Even in his operas melodies lend themselves to the discipline and poise of classical instrumental patterns; they do not endanger symphonic orderliness by wayward and impulsive transition. The typical instrumental theme is willing to be subjected to the requirements of symphonic law and logic; it will mingle on equal terms with other themes in a symphonic scheme; it will gladly serve simply as one strand amongst others in a symphonic texture. But poetic song is inclined to go ways of its own; it loves statement and repetition – the call and the echo from the volleying hills – but not always does it submit to formal preconceived development; at least, not Schubert's melody. That is why his instrumental music is happiest in its expositions and recapitulations, not in the working-out sections. And the whole point of a symphony is that there is a place and a time for transition and fresh ideas. Schubert was prone to be visited by a new lyric impulse in a coda. I am certain he was surprised, or rather enchanted, into composition. Mozart, on the contrary, knew what he was doing and where he was going. Schubert followed music like any child that ran after and with the Pied Piper. Counterpoint in abundance would have tripped him over in the dance down the primrose path. Nature, in fashioning Schubert, was wiser than his critics. Nature gave Schubert no more headwork than he needed.

When Liszt called Schubert the most poetic musician that ever lived, he showed a critical penetration most rare in an age in which the study of style in music remained rudimentary. I take it that Liszt meant that when Schubert composed he shaped his melody, coloured his harmony, arranged rhythm and modulation according to a mood or feeling strictly poetical – using the word poetical with the period's romantic implications. He did not draw his inspiration wholly from the nature of music, from a rapt contemplation of or absorption in the stuff and forms of music; the musical pattern was shaped by the poetic impulse. Mozart, even when he was at his most dramatic, began his work from a musician's delighted sense and observance of the forms of instrumental music as he knew them. No matter how often the fact is stated, it is not sufficiently realized that there are as many styles of musical as there are of poetic or verbal diction. There is the classical verse, the lyric verse, the blank verse, and the prose of music. There are composers of pellucid statement, and there are composers richly metaphorical. Schubert is always lyrical, romantic and metaphorical. There are few metaphors in Mozart; he is Augustan. Beethoven is a composer in molten prose; Wagner's greatest rhetoric is in blank verse. The verse conventions of the sublime style of the eighteenth century are honoured by Handel and Dryden alike. Schubert belongs entirely to poetry, moreover to the homely poetry of nature seen and felt in a flash under the conditions of his milieu. It is often said in disparagement of Schubert's taste for poetry that he was as happy setting Müller as he was setting Goethe to music; probably he was

happier, if ever he stayed to think about it. Müller was born
to write verses for Schubert, who would have written verses
of much the same kind had he been a poet and not a composer. Schubert could rise to the height of his theme when
he tackled Goethe; but only because of a mysterious divina-
tion of genius. Schubert was not a thinker and seldom if
ever a philosopher. That a boy was able to set the 'Erlkönig'
to music, once and for all, is not beyond explanation. The
'Erlkönig' is a dramatic poem, and it is as natural for eigh-
teen to be dramatic as it is for seventy, perhaps more so.
But reason becomes helpless when it seeks to account for
Schubert's insight into the 'Wilhelm Meister' songs. Still,
for all his astounding intuition, he could not take the
measure of the Harper of Goethe as completely as Wolf.
The greatest songs of Schubert may not be in the Müller
cycles; I am bold enough, though, to say that Schubert at
his greatest and profoundest and most psychological is not
Schubert at his most lovable and natural. In the simple
Müller verses he found a spring of sentiment and a turn for
the picturesque altogether after his heart and instincts. It
may indeed be said that for the creation of the two lovely
worlds of the 'Müllerin' and the 'Winterreise' cycles,
Schubert scarcely needed his genius at all. To discuss these
songs as the outcome of conscious art might well seem
ponderous and crude. Wolf's more imposing art can be
critically surveyed, and to some length accounted for, in
terms of cause and effect, in terms of a culture and a
sensibility and an imagination working with a technique in
a period ready for Wolf's genius. Schubert in his most
natural moments – and we find them in the Müller settings
abundantly – is no more a subject for analysis than the dew
on the flowers, or the tear on the lovesick miller's cheek.
That Schubert could forget, for the purpose of Müller's
verses, the range and power of expression and technique

which years earlier had produced 'Kennst du das Land' and 'Wer nie sein Brod' is only one amongst many mysteries in the art of this marvellous youth, who from his general appearance, chubby face and spectacles, might easily have been a sort of Tim Linkinwater of music, instead of 'le plus poète'.

III

There are, of course, poets and poets. Schubert was a poet of the heart, not of the passions. He wore his romantic rue with a difference – that is, when he wore rue of his own at all. He showed none of the symptoms which went with the period's diverse outbreaks of romanticism; he had neither the egoistic despair and disgust of Werther nor the heroics and arrogance of Childe Harold. He sought neither the solitude of melancholy eating out her heart nor did he trail a robe of woe theatrically for the world to see. He did not beat his breast in secret, and he did not strike an attitude, complete with cloak, on any public crag. He knew as little of 'les illusions perdues' as of Weltschmerz. He lacked pity of self or cynicism for life in general. When sorrow comes into his music it is not that sorrow which is born of worn years; it is the quick instinctive solicitude for all suffering creatures. Schubert is never sorry for himself. And he is never bitter, never renouncing or withdrawing. His heart wells out like healing friendliness to the pitiful 'Hurdy Gurdy Man'; he will go with him and share his unhappy songs; he is made happy and resilient through his own loving-kindness. For Schubert is always resilient; he is easily pleased; there is usually the upward movement and animation of youth in his music somewhere, a ripple of quavers and triplets, even though the surface is as frozen as the ice in the 'Winterreise' for a brief space. Compare Schubert's 'Prometheus' with Wolf's. The one is confident and young and unchained and free. C major, with all its brightness, crowns the end. Wolf gives us a Prometheus noble with scorn, but it is almost a pathological case. So with the two composers' treatment of Mignon. Schubert does not deprive her of simplicity and youth; Wolf sees her through the sad eyes of experience; he depicts an intense Mignon: another case for the nerve specialist.

It was in nature, fresh found, that Schubert sweetened his romanticism. Not a nature inimical, or inviting submergence of self in infinitude. Schubert's wind and rain and storm and snow are friendly really; gemütlich. Walk from Grinzing down to Vienna, even nowadays, and you will feel in the air, whatever the weather, the sense of that homely genius which presided finally over Schubert's art. We could almost call him a naive composer but for his wonderful craftsmanship. He is a fair example of the 'pathetic fallacy' of Ruskin; he identifies his moods with those of nature. And he is always his own hero. When the miller's heart is happy, very well then; all the countryside is happy too, birds in the air, flowers, and the heaven, the earth, and the waters under the earth. But as soon as disaster comes and snaps the heart, then the sun mocks, and the weathercock taunts, and the snows of the year are as the snows of his hair.

Schubert in the 'Müllerin' and 'Winterreise' cycles (I take them as instances; but any other of his finest songs would serve as well) does not keep apart from his theme; he has none of the detachment of Wolf, whose irony is conscious art, tinctured with the bitter-sweet of an observer of the tragi-comedy of things. Wolf would not have written 'Das Wandern' without giving us some subtle hint of the wrath to come. The irony that moves us in Schubert, if we contemplate the two cycles as a whole – which we should – is an irony which we can say almost with certainty was not deliberately connived by Schubert. But when we look back from the numb misery of 'Der Leiermann' at the end of the 'Winterreise' to the blithe carefree ardour of the young miller who set out on his travels light of heart in 'Das Wandern', how exquisitely we are wounded, all the more so because it is a wound that hurts without malice aforethought. Schubert never points an acid moral.

> Fancy, who leads the pastimes of the glad
> Full oft is pleased a wayward dart to throw;
> Sending sad shadows after things not sad.

Much has been made of Schubert's saying that he composed his songs out of his sorrows. The point is that as soon as he began to compose he ceased to be sorrowful. 'I live and compose like a god', he wrote in a letter of 1818. He was rather like a young god, serving an apprenticeship in the godlike and not yet qualified to hurl spiteful thunderbolts at the wicked world. You can see him and the other young gods at play in the scherzo of the C major Symphony, tossing the rainbow ball of music about and stretching the growing limbs. How could a mortal man be unhappy for long whose heart knew Schubert's unending melody? Possibly he would have been called an escapist had he lived at the present time and composed as he did. The modern way of treating the jilted hero of 'Die schöne Müllerin' would immerse him neck-high in a bog of the latest psychology, and make him sticky with sex. Schubert's rippling brook would be transformed into the stagnant pool of the closing scene of *Wozzeck*. The fashions of life change, indeed. Schubert performs a miracle with Müller's verses. He identifies himself with their content, absorbs the 'emotional stuff', then takes it into another dimension, so to say. The world of 'Die schöne Müllerin', and of Schubert generally, is real without being rational. Today it is easy, if we forget the art, to regard the forlorn swain of Müller and Schubert as the

21

faded poetic fashion of a period. But in a hundred years from now the current sophistry about complexes, criticism of life, and the rest will have become faded and 'period' as well. The ethic, the metaphysic, the attitude or experience, will survive only if beauty is conjured out of it. The sorrows of Goethe's Werther are to modern readers almost as laughably mannered as those of Müller's hero. In Goethe's day – which at least was as intelligent as ours – Werther set a fashion in disillusion and pessimism that swept the Continent and was taken seriously by a man of Napoleon's sense of fact. If *Werther* is no longer worth our while as literature – and I do not say it is not – it is because the genius in it was never vital enough, not because the view of life expressed has become 'old-fashioned'. Of course it has; there is no permanence in any age's interpretation of existence. Only the art, the thing created, lasts. Müller meant as much to Schubert, let us make no mistake, as Wedekind meant to the Alban Berg of *Lulu*. Only the foolish mind imagines that it is necessary to insist that the arts should serve as an interpretation of or a reaction to the 'modern world', as the cant phrase has it. Where is the realism today of Zola which seemed to many folk so very real not long ago? 'Beauty is truth, truth beauty.' Keats and Schubert said it almost simultaneously, though, as Gretchen might lisp, 'in rather different words'.

If we are moved nearly to tears at, say, Schubert's setting of 'Thränenregen', the cause of the emotion is not wholly or even mainly the hero's ill-starred lot, though as I have tried to suggest, we can easily overdo a patronizing point of view towards the 'old-fashioned'. Schubert most times transcended his theme. He who could begin to compose from a pictorial idea, on the verge of the imitative ('Gretchen am Spinnrade') invariably soared to another plane of reality, the reality of pure imagination, which is a different plane from that of dramatic or representative expression. He was the reed through which all blew not so much to music as to song. His symphonies are song symphonies which had to wait for Brahms to render properly symphonic.

It was the spontaneous and swift impulse of lyricism that left him frequently with little or no time to attend diligently to every verbal value in his text – accentuation and what not. With Wolf, who was the greatest of dramatic and psychological song writers, words and music were one and indivisible in a transcript of life and nature. A particular verbal significance, even a particular verbal accent, meant volumes to Wolf. That is why he needed to treat accentuation in a setting with much more than Schubert's care. If you do not know the words of a Wolf song in detail you will miss perhaps more than half of the music's point and fine art. In Schubert a knowledge of the title of the lyric, or a generalized notion of the poetic intent, will many times (though of course not always) amply prepare the imagination for the music's power. Words with Schubert were necessary as a ground-plan is necessary in the erection of a beautiful building; but he went far beyond the dimensional world of the 'blueprint'. The magic of 'Thränenregen' (one of the most rare and marvellous of songs, even in Schubert) is subtly compounded of the pictorial, the present scene and sentiment, and reflection. Most important of all, the song, for all its appeal as a story, a picture, and a colloquy between lovers, is absolutely lyrical. The night's peacefulness can be felt in every bar; the miller's devotion is expressed, the modulation when the maid shyly says 'Es kommt ein Regen' is a piece of exact character drawing – yet everything is done and suggested in terms of pure song. What touches us most is a melody that is not dependent on, though it is evoked by, the particular scene or emotion. Schubert's imagination had little of Wolf's protean power.

He entered the various worlds of his poets, but he subdued them to his own realms of song. Compare his setting of Goethe's Harper songs with Wolf's; Schubert cannot be bitter, cannot break our hearts or fill us with protest against the heavenly powers; Schubert provides the anodyne of beauty. He is less true to Goethe maybe; but he had first of all to listen to his own muse, the lyrical muse, who is jealous but stays for ever with those who are true to her.

I have mentioned the pictorial aspect of much of Schubert's song. The term must not be misunderstood; Schubert is seldom if ever pictorial or atmospheric in the obvious sense of these terms. He sees with the eyes of poetry and hears with the ears of music. Beethoven maintained that his 'Pastoral' Symphony was more feeling than painting. We shall go farther later in this book into the distinction between vision and seeing in music; here I wish only to point out that Beethoven in the 'Pastoral' makes the sounds of bird life and of rain and thunder and lightning. Schubert avoids the onomatopoeic even when he is at his most vividly pictorial. To take a simple example, he lets us see the tail of a fish flicking in 'Die Forelle'; it is suggested by a figure which purely as music is delightful and satisfying; anybody hearing the song and not knowing what it was all about would feel at once the charm of the figure strictly as a motif. Then on being told that it was not only exquisite music but also most apt pictorialism, how the wonder and joy would increase! Two sides of our aesthetic sensibility are enchanted by Schubert's ability to present all things, his view of the external universe and his spirit's absorption in it, in terms of music that is simply bursting to be sung, whether Lied, trio, quartet, quintet and octet, or symphony.

IV

There is a quality or characteristic of Schubert's music not often remarked upon, yet it throws a light into the essence of his style and order of imagination. I know of no composer whose music so consistently gives us the sense of wandering motion. Schubert is never still; always he is setting out on a journey. I am not referring, of course, simply to tempo or rhythm, considered in the abstract; I mean that Schubert expresses persistently an idea and feeling of wandering motion. Mozart moves, but not as a wanderer waiting to be led; Mozart's motion is that of the spheres in their pre-destined rotation. Rossini goes so fast that he achieves the immobility of a top spinning round and round in the same direction. Beethoven climbs and assaults summits, when he is not withdrawn to the still silent session of meditation. Wagner swims. But Schubert, being a vagrant composer, hesitates at the beginning of most of his greater works, as though before a finger-post; they nearly all start from a 'Wegweiser'; and a finger-post is suggestive, not conclusive. It does not draw a map of the landscape to scale. The ordnance survey shows you how to get there; the finger-post, with more imagination, merely points into the distance. Schubert was fascinated all his life with a 'Wanderer' motif; sometimes it takes the form of a carefree movement or gait onward through the fields and by the streams; some-times it is a tread of twilight resignation such as we hear in the pizzicato of the adagio of the C major Quintet, or it is a hushed expectant venturing into the allegro of the B minor Symphony where we can well believe Schubert was stricken with awe out of his senses by the new world he had come across; or the journey onward is changed by unseen forces to the stamping of the finale of the C major Symphony. There is always a digression in Schubert; he did not care for the main roads. As Donald Tovey in more scholarly language puts it, Schubert did not always remember that the time for an exposition of themes is not the time for discursive treatment of them. He conjured from nowhere the first romantic symphony – Austrian, not German; and also he romanticized[1] chamber music. It is not, after all, difficult to understand how, given his genius, he could without need of additional miracles compose his songs. The soil for his songs had been tilled for him. But where did he hear for the first time the sound of the Schubert orchestra, a sound unlike any before, with horns and trombones and woodwind opening magic casements? Weber had caught the same strains but he could not follow them and break free from the theatre of stage magic of his German day. Weber's forest of romance turns out to be theatre property after all. Schubert brought a quiver of sensibility to the symphony and even left far behind him the familiar and companionable atmosphere of the landscape and city that bred him.

In the G major Quartet, known as his Op. 161, we find with an even more unmistakable poignancy than in the 'Unfinished' Symphony, the C major Quintet or the C major Symphony, the intimations and the 'still fair hopes' which lie entombed in the Friedhof of Vienna in a grove of cypress. There are here beautiful ideas, boldness and bigness of reach and grasp, an entirely new chamber harmony with chords rich and romantic in themselves and not the necessary and logical outcome of the part-writing. Elegy and the grotesque; Ländler and Dance of Death; sublimity and song; music in garlands and in tangled growths.

The wanderer in the end wandered far out of sight of his gemütlich Vienna; he walked in woods different from the Wienerwald; he entered the magic woods of Westermain. He vagabonded beyond the friendly Kahlenberg which looks

[1] There is no other word, much as I dislike it.

26

down on Vienna. He reached the upper slopes of Olympus.
It was no track that had been followed before; even the
finger-posts didn't guess it. Poetry discovered the way,
poetry and song – temporarily visiting the earth in the
shape and habiliments, spectacles and all, of one baptized
Franz Peter Seraph.

II
Wagner
1813-1883

Wagner

ERNEST NEWMAN once said to me, with appropriate gravity: 'You know, as a music-critic you labour under a serious disadvantage.' I wondered what awful deficiency his penetrating eye had found in my aesthetic and technical equipment; and I quakingly said: 'Yes, please ... what is it?' 'You *like* music, my dear man, actually like it. It will be the ruin of you.'

The circumstance that prompted Newman's remark was peculiar. In May 1933, when I had passed my forty-third birthday and should have known better, I was obliged to leave a performance of *Walküre* at the Covent Garden Opera before the end, because the hour was late and I had to write a column notice for my paper. When I came out of the darkened theatre in the squalor of Bow Street, the contrast of reality to the splendour of Wagner's remote world was too much for me. I lost my bearings in the labyrinth of Long Acre and environs, and when at last I returned to sanity I discovered myself a mile from where I should have been.

I suppose that this performance of *Walküre* was the fiftieth I had heard, or thereabouts. I went through the young man's Wagnerianism in the years of 1905-10; the star of Wagner was high in the sky, and into our ken flashed the comet Strauss; we hailed it as such, at any rate. By the time 1933 arrived, and long before that, Wagner had been 'dispossess'd, chuck'd down', the tricks of Klingsor had lost their power. Young bloods (if blood any of them possessed at all, or indeed, would have confessed to possessing) looked down their noses at Wagner, despising his art of 'gesture', of musical 'histrionics', as the better-read of them put it, echoing Nietzsche's reaction; the others used the old tags, 'decadent', or 'otiose', or 'rhetorical'. Then came Hitler, and in Wagner the whole credo of Nazism was discerned by the chosen people, those who now heard themselves called to represent the highest-browed standards of taste. Siegfried and the sword; the crash and surge of the Wagnerian orchestra ... besides, had not Wagner written the vile *Judenthum in der Musik*? Hitler, it was rumoured, admired *Lohengrin*; so much for Wagner. But even serious musicians aspired to rise superior to the Wagner scores; this they averred, was fabricated composition, dependent on mechanical sequences. Wagner was a swimmer tossed on the seas of his own orchestra, plunging towards any island of a set-piece, ensemble, even an aria, blowing out his hot air. 'If you are young', writes Professor Dent, 'and have never seen it [the 'Ring'], it may still be one of the great experiences of your life.' If you are young! Ah, the change of fashion during the years! I can remember when it was as necessary to be a Wagnerian, if you would cherish aspirations towards the circles of the highest culture, as now it is to swear by Busoni, or (if you are English) by Vaughan Williams or folk-dancing. Not only the music of Wagner but his poetry and 'philosophy' were deemed essential to the general cosmic scheme that was Wagner. Today there is none so poor to do him reverence, except apparently Ernest Newman and myself. Both of us can even turn a blind eye on certain of Wagner's unmistakable excesses and excrescences. If you point out to me that Wagner is occasionally, even often, tedious; that he achieves a longitude that staggers the heart; that his metaphysic is not the metaphysic a 'modern world' (whatever a 'modern world' may be) can accept; if also you draw attention to the want of poise and restraint

in much of his music, to his frequent obviousness, to his
swollen orchestration here and there, to his inflexibility of
rhythm more than here and there (four in a bar, two
crotchets, a dotted crotchet, and a quaver); well, I shall
probably not only agree with your catalogue of Wagner's
'defects', but will undertake to add one or two other shortcomings which you may well not be acquainted with. Look
into any artist's work for traits of style which do not belong
to it, traits of style which the artist, because of his particular
temperament, could not possibly show; look for these irrelevances, and then, if you have taken the care to approach
the work in question with a personal dislike of its style, why,
you will be able to condemn it easily enough, according to
your lights. Schiller, in a letter to Goethe, wrote of a criticism delivered on 'Wilhelm Meister' by a certain Jacobi:
'Jacobi is one of those who seek only their own ideas in the
representation of poets, and prize more what *should be* than
what *is* ... So soon as a man lets me see that there is anything in poetical representation that interests him more
than internal necessity and truth, I give him up.'

When I reeled out of Covent Garden Opera on that warm
night of May twenty-four years ago, I think I knew my
Wagner as intimately as any of his detractors, or deflators,
confidentially so-called. To say the truth, I have not for
years willingly attended a performance of the 'Ring'; my
spirit groans and protests at the thought of Fricka and
Wotan and their arguments; at the thought of the riddles
of the Wanderer; at the thought of the barkings and snar-
lings of Alberich; at the thought of the whinings of Mime.
But only in advance do these fears afflict me; as soon as
Wagner begins his work I am placed under an enchantment.
Let me say at once that it is no eye of a rattlesnake that fixes
me ('the old rattlesnake', as Nietzsche said of Wagner, after
the reaction). The factor in Wagner that perpetually

fascinates me is the music, to which I attend with an ear that, I hope, knows what music should be *qua* music; but I also attend with that other ear, which will freely work in conjunction with the strict musician's ear, the ear of imagination. In other words, I have learned to listen to Wagner much as a scholar and poet might listen to Shakespeare; his ear instinctively, from long and close knowledge of the text, appreciating the poetry *qua* cunningly contrived prosody, but also absorbing at the same time the great and human overtones of the drama.

Thus is the Wagnerian nowadays compelled to give evidence that he listens to the music not entirely as one who is an out-of-date romantic nurtured in the nineteenth century. I am certain that I could have persuaded even Constant Lambert or W. J. Turner to read this essay to the end had I refrained from mentioning a single character in Wagner, or a single emotional significance; if, instead, I had concentrated on Wagner's musical structure, on his form and physiology, the way he develops a scene symphonically, sometimes observing A-B-A divisions, and all the rest of it. (For an example of a musical structure of this order, study the monologue of Mime at the beginning of Act I of *Siegfried*. I choose this instance at random from many that come to mind.)

I happen, though, to be writing my essay for my own pleasure, and from a wish, first of all, to pay a tribute in these days to Wagner the artist, who has given me experiences in music and in imaginative living equal to any I have known of their kind. ('Of their kind', mark you.)

II

The mind of Wagner worked on two planes. He saw with his ears and heard with his eyes. Isolde waves her scarf; and we hear it in the orchestra. Mime seeks how to forge the sword, and we are shown the interior of his dark primitive mind (the wood-wind at the beginning of *Siegfried*, Act I); Kurwenal looks out on the vacant waste of the sea for a sign of Isolde's ship. And the rising string harmonies tell us that his eyes scan the horizon and find nothing. We hear vacancy. Beckmesser suddenly discovers a new song by Hans Sachs; the orchestra also sees it, at the precise moment that Beckmesser's attention is attracted to the table. Wagner, of a truth, composed with many eyes, many ears, many hands; he weaves his orchestral tissue on many shuttles. He looks backward and forward at the same time; a binding strand here, another there; a gathering up of the skein; a great unravelling of it; the needles flash, endlessly. But the simile of the shuttle and the weaver will not do; it is not dynamic – or as Falstaff would say, not forgetive – enough. Rather let us think of the forces of growth themselves, the seminal energy of the earth, beginning from the upheavals which threw up mountains and at the same time achieved the quietest flower and the peace of a spring night. For Wagner is not always in the 'Ring' hurling a hammer in the world's forge; he has noble condescensions and yieldings. There is a Freia as well as Fafner and Fasolt. The string music, when Sieglinde bends over the weary Siegmund in Act I of *Walküre*, is in the style of the miniature; it is chamber music pure and simple. In all the stormy purpled passion of *Tristan*, the honest open-as-the-day manliness of Kurwenal comes as the sane air into a doomed drugged universe.

Wagner's art, I admit, is so potent that occasionally we are persuaded against our better reasoning. After all, what *is* the significance to us of all these gods, and potion-drinkers, and dwarfs, and river-nymphs, and battle-maidens? In *Tristan*, is it Schopenhauer or the love-draught; metaphysics or stage magic? Where in all this pantomimery is that criticism of life which is the stuff of great art? Wagner gives us little time to think; he takes us by the scruff of the neck and hurls us into his world. The point is that whether you like it or not it *is* a world, peopled and alive. You may find them all boring, objectionable, monstrous, sentimentally or heroically Teutonic; none the less, you cannot deny that they do exist – Wotan, Brünnhilde, Sieglinde, Siegmund, Alberich, Mime, Tristan, Isolde, Brangäne, Marke, Kurwenal, Hans Sachs, David, Beckmesser, Walther; they are all as real in imaginative art as anybody in Shakespeare. That is, I think, undeniable. And the Wagner who could create a gallery of beings, human and sub-human and godlike, by his music; the Wagner who, according to Bernard Shaw, could not write absolute music to save his life, this same Wagner is the only composer of opera whose music can be presented in the concert hall and there appeal to thousands who have never seen the music-dramas. Imagine a concert programme of 'excerpts' from Verdi. Wagner hated a concert performance of his music torn from its dramatic context; the fact remains that his music has for years stood the test of performance under conditions where it has to be listened to as absolute music. It is proof of the essentially musical character and structure of Wagner's art that it can survive separation from stage action and the dramatic context. Herein is the wonder of the man; he could create by music his different worlds and the inhabitants of them: Nibelheim, Nürnberg, Isolde's garden; and he could compose music fit to be listened to symphonically.

My argument that Wagner was essentially a musical genius, as musical as Bach himself, does not go so far as to share the common belittlement of him as a dramatic writer. There are superb strokes of characterization in Wagner, considered as drama. There are living and diverse people who sometimes have pertinent things to say. Marke's 'Mir dies? Dies, Tristan, mir?' is absolutely right; there is nothing in Goethe more apt and moving. We are not so very far from Lear's 'Pray you, undo this button' when Isolde leans over the dying Tristan and cries 'Die Wunde – wo?' Or when, on the rising wave of the Liebestod, she exhorts Marke, Brangäne and the others: 'Seht ihr's Freunde?' If we are not here in the realms of absolute drama and poetry, then I do not know what is the substance of these arts. No merely clever versifier, a maker of libretti for music, chopping up prose into convenient rhythms and lengths, could have given us Brünnhilde's lines, warning Siegmund of his approaching end: 'Nur Todgeweihten taugt mein Anblick.' Hofmannsthal was considered one of Central Europe's finest poets and writers for the theatre. As comedy pure and self-subsistent, the text of *Rosenkavalier* is not in any way superior to that of *Meistersinger*. Hans Sachs's

> Nur sang er, wie er musst'
> Und wie er musst' so konnt er

is perfect. Wotan's cadence

> Denn so kehrt der Gott sich dir ab
> So küsst er die Gottheit von dir

is genuine dramatic poetry.

Any artist writing strictly in dramatic and theatre values would be glad to be visited by ideas and inspirations such as the sudden opening of the door of the dwelling of Hunding, at the height of the love duet of Sieglinde and Siegmund; none but a born dramatist could have penetrated so intensely as this the scene and the action, so intensely that he visualized not only the immediate and present human interest but also was alive to all the surrounding and hidden impersonal forces – the wind and the silent moonlit night outside, and to the prosaic fact that as there was a hinge on the door of the hut, it could be blown open. Here is the comprehensive imagination of truly dramatic art.

If I were a dramatist of the theatre pure and simple, I would be proud of a conception and technique as vivid and simple as Wagner's, where at the height of the scene with the Flower Maidens we hear the call of Kundry: 'Parsifal—weile.'

Consider, too, the silence at the beginning of Act I of *Tristan* immediately after the curtain has risen and we have heard the bodeful plucked notes of suspense of the double-basses; then the voice of the sailor up in the masts and sails. No other opera and few plays have begun as originally and as powerfully as this. It is not to the point to say that the stuff of poetry and drama in Wagner needed the life-giving warmth and energy of his music; the gist of the matter is that Wagner the composer was able to nourish his art on great and inflammable dramatic conceptions. His despised stagecraft achieved magnificent theatre, time after time.

Wagner's was a mind compact of music, yet needing changeful life and emotion to shape and enliven the forms of his music; for music must have form and logical transition of its own; it cannot run after dramatic action and sequence. Other composers find inspiration in the forms which strictly belong to music; they dramatize adagios and allegros, contrasts of key, and so on. Wagner the musician needed the urge from Wagner the dramatist, much as Shakespeare the poet welcomed the urge from Shakespeare the dramatist. If we were to strip the poetry from the plays of Shakespeare is it certain he could emerge mountains higher than Wagner as a playwright? Let us give the devil his due; the habit of decrying Wagner as a dramatist has even persuaded many Wagnerians (I was amongst them myself not long ago) to contemplate sadly a Wagner who was caught up like Laocoön in an entanglement of theatre claptrap, verbosity, alliteration, pantomimery and what not. He should have lived hereafter, they say; then he would have found the language of music already pregnant with self-contained significances fit to express a contemporary feeling about life and destiny. Mr Newman has toyed with the idea of the symphony Wagner might have composed. Wagner himself lived long enough to make music fruitful; he endowed it with a continuous plastic movement and logic. If only he had lived later – would he not have dispensed with the scaffolding of words and plot? Then the cloud-capped and gorgeous palaces would have gone up by the conjuration of music alone. The 'Siegfried' Idyll was a portent.

All of which argument seems to me as though we should deplore that Shakespeare did not devote himself always to sonnets and other forms of absolute poetry. Wagner was a musician working in the theatre exactly as Shakespeare was a poet working in the theatre. His main problem was to make music dramatic and symphonic at one and the same time. His aesthetic and indeed the structural foundation and security of his vast conceptions demanded an organic instrumental tissue which would observe a strictly musical logic, with transition and contrast of rhythm and form achieving balance and independent life and power. It was necessary for him to write his own libretti to get within reach of an aim so desirable and so immensely in advance of the period in which he began to change opera, with its set and purely instrumental forms, into music-drama. For it is not possible to compose an organic music tissue to words and action conceived independently as drama. Wagner realized (as another German realized before Wagner was born) that music does not naturally wed itself to stage drama. Music is mainly an art of emotional expression; the poet or librettist should therefore make his text musical in shape and contrast of mood, and especially in the rise and fall of emotional tempo and tension. Obviously music cannot move and make its transitions as quickly as words and a realistic stage action; an Oscar Wilde dialogue, or the intellectual content of a play by Bernard Shaw, would render music tongue-tied and inarticulate. The ideal opera libretto should contain nothing that does not lend itself to the rhythm and the general ebb and flow and rise and fall of music. Wagner almost achieved this ideal in the text of *Tristan*; but by the fact of the different laws and nature of music and drama a consistent fusion of the two, in a long work, is apparently not possible. A stage play cannot live entirely on emotional stuff, on the material of music; there are plot-circumstances to be made clear. Even in *Tristan* there are inevitably periods during which the music merely marks time during a stretch of description or explanation; we have to be told certain bald facts even in a text which in Wagner's own words reduced to a minimum 'the copious detail which an historical poet has to employ in order to make the outer connections of his plot evident'. In the libretto of *Tristan*, Wagner maintained, he 'immersed himself in the depths of soul-events pure and simple, and from out of this innermost centre of the world fearlessly fashioned its outward form'.... But not quite.

With the vaster canvas of the 'Ring' he could not of course achieve a continuous fusion of music and stage action and words – and we may safely say that if Wagner found the task now and then beyond him no other composer is likely ever to succeed, where he only was half triumphant, in solving an insoluble problem of aesthetics.

But it was a failure which we must measure by the vast ends envisaged by Wagner – the creation of a music that would go beyond music, a music which while retaining its own forms and tone-appeal, would become fertilized from life, from the human-all-too-human, and even from the superhuman.

Less than forty years after the composition of the Ninth Symphony of Beethoven, Wagner composed *Tristan*. A new texture of sound, a new significance, a new instrumentation, a new vocal melody; a new musical psychology – and a music that not only was potent in itself, as music, but one which changed ways of life, ways of conceiving love and death. To this day, more than seventy years after his death, and after the production of thousands of volumes discussing his art, the truth is still only faintly grasped that Wagner was primarily a composer of music, a maker and shaper of organic musical forms, as intently observing the essential nature and laws of music while creating Hans Sachs and Brünnhilde as Shakespeare was a poet intently observing the essential qualities and laws of poetry and prose while creating Falstaff and Cleopatra.

III

He laid aside the 'Ring' in 1857, and calmly proceeded to compose *Tristan*. Then he turned to the world of *Meistersinger*; two works as different as night from day; the one glorifies, in fact, night and death, the other glorifies life and day. The miracle of it! – to interrupt *Siegfried* and to think himself into the shot-silk tragedy of *Tristan und Isolde*; then to think himself into the radiant sunshine of the greatest of comedies in music; not only the genius but the effrontery of it. You do not juggle with masterpieces, like a Cinquevalli, keeping three of them going at once, one up, t'other come down. He interrupted his work on *Siegfried* in the second act, where Siegfried rests under the trees; not for a dozen years did Wagner again pick up the score of *Siegfried*, but when at last he did pick it up he wrote and imagined from the place, the very bar, exactly where he had left off, took up the identical strands in the orchestral tissue and began again to weave the great fabric of the 'Ring' ... and nobody today can place his finger on the score of Act II of *Siegfried* and show the point of interruption; there is no 'joint', no hiatus, no caesura of style; for Wagner transformed his whole being as artist and technician back to the old legendary universe of gods and dragons and wood-birds. He had, as he said, 'ripped Siegfried from my heart', put him under lock and key, 'like someone that one buries alive'. Then Wagner voyaged in a distant, 'ein fremdes Land', where the sun never shone, 'das dunkel nächt'ge Land'. He completed *Tristan* in 1859, emerged from the purple chromaticism of the tragedy of passion to the genial diatonics of one of the most spacious and triumphant of all announcements of the worthiness of man and his humours. And so thoroughly was the dyer's hand 'subdued to that it worked in' that when Hans Sachs quotes a bar or two from *Tristan* it is as though a dark and alien stain falls on the sunny texture of *Meistersinger*. The paradox is that the style in both *Tristan* and *Meistersinger* is, bar by bar, constantly Wagner's and nobody else's. It is not, as Nietzsche somewhere contemptuously remarks, a case of histrionics, of 'acting'. Wagner does not put on a *Tristan* make-up, then discard it for another and external disguise when he comes to *Meistersinger*. The two universes of these operas are created from within, projected outwards, from the heart of Wagner's imagination. Mozart shared something of the same protean genius, of course; but he was born before his time; he lacked the wider dramatic vocabulary, the more plastic material, which music had developed by the time Wagner was ready. With a few changes of harmony, simple to a first-year composition class, Mozart creates the sublimity of Sarastro. We must bow the head before art as evocative as this. But the range of dramatic contrast in Mozart's day was limited, because the problem had not been seriously tackled then of where the scope of instrumental music ended and that of opera began. Don Giovanni sings a serenade which would seem quite at home if transposed for soprano voice and given to Zerlina. The wonderful beginning of the finale of Act II of *Figaro* ('Esci omai') does not take us entirely away from the instrumental style of, say, the first movement of the 'Prague' Symphony.

I do not wish to exaggerate Wagner's genius for clear-cut characterization. I do not say that David in *Meistersinger* could not, without incongruity, sing a bar of Walther's music; no doubt these two parts could interchange here and there phrases of quasi-recitative, if a dovetailing of the verbal text could also be contrived. But imagine David and Walther interchanging their trial songs; imagine the naive phrases of David's 'Am Jordan Sankt Johannes stand' coming from the throat of Walther, or Walther's passionate but aristocratically lyrical 'Am stillen Herd' coming from David's youthful throat. Yet if Wagner in his comedy differentiates between knight and apprentice, between high born and lowly born, giving them for truth's sake music of a contrasted idiom and poise, there is no favouring of class or degree in the distribution of Wagner's genius on one and all. Into every nook and cranny of Wagner's Nürnberg vitality shines like the sun, endowing everybody with life, pride of movement, contagious humanity. The Mastersingers are not more abundantly alive than their apprentices; in this great comedy Jack is at least as good as his master. The Nightwatchman passes only twice across the stage, blowing his horn, but he is as richly blessed with creative genius as Hans Sachs himself and as he passes across the scene of sleeping Nürnberg, he remains in our mind gratefully for ever. Flaubert said of the *Comédie*

Humaine of Balzac that in it even the scullions possess genius. So with *Meistersinger*: nobody has been stinted of vitality or kept out of the radiant warmth which is Wagner's creative touch, kindly, wise, tender and strong. Beckmesser is not spitefully treated really; at the end Wagner persuades our sympathies towards his pitiful posturings and emulations of the romantic lyrist. The point is that Beckmesser is as much charged with creative power as Sachs and the rest of them.

In *Meistersinger*, again, we feel the sense of the two-planed genius of Wagner; music here has eyes as well as ears. The characters are drawn from within; every note sung by Hans Sachs matches the man's appearance; music is the source of his physical being; out of music he is born. Yet the characters are also observed from the outside; they are photographed as well as psychologized (if I may use a hideous but convenient word); so that when Beckmesser, after the mêlée in the streets at midnight, comes next day into the house of Sachs, we are not only taken into his mind, to share his self-pity, his rage, and his cunning; the music mirrors as well his every anguished movement. When the pain of a bruise twists his back abruptly, the orchestra reveals it to us. This art is not merely ingenious instrumental onomatopoeia; it is art that absolutely absorbs its subject or theme, soul and body.

As the Rhine runs through the 'Ring', or remains near enough to the action to serve as a sort of *deus ex machina* in nature, waiting its bodeful cue, so is medieval Nürnberg omnipresent in *Meistersinger*; we know that tragedy cannot occur in a place so gracious, so far-removed from the complicated highway of affairs. At one moment, true, Wagner goes far beyond the locale, beyond his immediate theme. Hans Sachs dwells on the wild doings that happened on Midsummer's Eve. In a flash of vision, Sachs (or rather Wagner) sees in Nürnberg's momentary madness a microcosm of the greater world 'Wahn! Wahn! überall Wahn!' For some reason, men begin to fight one another. God knows how it happens – this cry of Sachs ('Gott weiss wie das geschah') is one of the most profoundly moving and human that ever came from the soul of an artist, and also it is one of the prophetic moments of art. The whole of this 'Wahn! Wahn!' monologue is an extraordinary instance of an artist building more wisely than he suspected. Wagner, we know, was at all times ready to delay the action of a scene, given half a chance to philosophize. I doubt whether he guessed that the 'Wahn! Wahn!' monologue would one day express, in its wise sad mingled perplexity, its resignation, and its will-to-do-better, the inarticulate spirit of our present age. In the heart-swelling crescendo, Sachs says: 'Come, let us see what can be done to shape things to a better end', and we hear the Nürnberg motif. The subtlest of all artists, life itself, has beaten the best in irony of all the published comedians. Hitler, it came to pass, chose Nürnberg; and where Hans Sachs sang, he spoke. 'Gott weiss wie das geschah!'

Comedy must transcend its immediate object, which is to stir thoughtful laughter. Somehow it should, in its warm genial rays, show us some of the world's dust; not by conscious intent will the artist of comedy let shadows of mortality fall over his happy heaven's sun. If he is a great man, he will be visited by overtones, by premonitions which he would not be able to explain were he to pause to analyse them. It is the sensitive stuff of life in him that renders him an unwitting instrument, or a medium, for the expression of the recurring dissonances in human nature. Verdi's *Falstaff*, sparkling and ever-fresh work of an eighty-year-old genius, fails considered as the highest form of comedy, because there is in it no hint of irony or of criticism of life. Mozart, least philosophical of artists, was wiser than that; the ripple of wit, the comedy of manners supposedly artificial, is mortally shaded for a moment when the Countess sings 'Porgi Amor'.

IV

In a great comedy the creative energy must send out its rays right and left, giving or liberating life everywhere. Everything must happen to everybody taking part in the comedy, not only to the protagonists of the main theme. In tragedy, on the other hand, the imaginative energy concentrates, not spreads; it draws all things into its circle of obsession; for tragedy means obsession. The fire that consumes Tristan and Isolde and King Marke consumes Brangäne and the honest sane Kurwenal; they are each sucked into the centre of fate and doom. Even the Shepherd, in Act III, cannot call his soul his own; he exists only in so far as he is an aspect or reflection of the Tristan–Isolde tragedy; he is merely Tristan's eyes looking for the ship over the empty sea.

In *Meistersinger* all the men and the women are free individuals, free to live and love and laugh and weep according to private destiny. Not the whole of Nürnberg is wrapped up in the fate of Walther and Eva; they are not more the chosen of God or Venus than David and Magdalena. Walther being weighed in the balance at the tournament of song is not a more important protagonist in the general scheme than Beckmesser. Hans Sachs carries his own secret sorrow. The apprentices enjoy souls of their own. A beautiful touch, which in a moment shows the beneficent hand of Wagner blessing with pride of life the smallest of his creatures, occurs in Act I, in the scene where the Mastersingers are assembling. Kothner calls out the names

'Veit Pogner?' 'Hier zur Hand', 'Kunz Vogelsang?' 'Ein sich fand.' Then he calls for Niklaus Vögel, and an apprentice jumps up in his seat at the back and cries out, 'Ist krank' – 'He is ill'. 'God send him recovery!' says Kothner; and the apprentice, with a respectful 'Schön Dank', sits down again. Simply that and nothing more. But he has had his moment; nay, he shares in the general immortality of the work. If I were a young singer, and the part given me in a performance of *Meistersinger* were merely Niklaus Vögel's apprentice, I would live through each day waiting impatiently to contribute my 'solos' – 'Ist krank' and 'Schön Dank'; for they come in the high-tide of an orchestral sea not excelled in Wagner for golden-flooded grandeur, all flowing from a four-note theme. How perfect the responses which ride on the current of this music; it is an antiphony of friendship:

> 'Hermann Ortel?'
>> 'Immer am Ort.'
> 'Balthasar Zorn?'
>> 'Bleibt niemals fort.'
> 'Konrad Nachtigall?'
>> 'Treu seinem Schlag.'
> 'Augustin Moser?'
>> 'Nie fehlen mag.'
> 'Niklaus Vögel ... Schweigt?'
>> 'Ist krank.'
> 'Gut' Bess'rung dem Meister Walt's Gott!'
>> 'Schön Dank!'

In a world that mainly has little time or opportunity to read, it is easy to get a wrong notion established by the simple practice of repeating it often enough. Wagner, the gossips declare, cannot abide restraint; he must needs declaim always at the top of his voice. Debussy somewhere

writes of the virtues of silence in music for the theatre: 'I
have used silence as a means of expression. Don't laugh.
It is perhaps the only means of bringing into relief the
emotional value of a phrase. If Wagner used silence at all
I should say it was only in an extremely dramatic way.' I
can appreciate the point of this subtle criticism by Debussy
of Wagner's treatment of orchestral dynamics; but I would
maintain that in music silence can be expressed without
resort to absence of sound, which is rather an evasion of the
problem. When Eva, in Act II of *Meistersinger* says to
Walther: 'Geliebter, spare den Zorn!' and we hear the
Nightwatchman's call, the whole and multitudinous orchestra of Wagner breathes silence, fragrant silence, silence of
summer night. Where is there a silence in music more
intent than that which we feel when Hans Sachs ponders
his problems in the 'Wie duftet doch' monologue? But I do
not set out to overrate qualities in Wagner which did not
belong to him. Silence, as Debussy understood silence, is
expressed at the beginning of *Pelléas*, in the sombre forest
where Golaud finds himself lost. Not by any obvious
abstaining from sound does Debussy evoke the silence of a
world not peopled by ordinary mortal stuff; the colour and
harmonies of the wood-wind, the triplets in violoncellos
and contrabasses, evoke the silence Debussy had in mind, a
silence which was his own secret and one that died with
him. You will hear it also at the beginning of the first song
of the 'Chansons de Bilitis': 'La Flûte de Pan'. But Wagner
was, in *Meistersinger*, a humanist, a man of German
humours, before he was a poet; and in that crowded animate
world the silence of things not familiar and palpable would
have seemed surely an artistic error. I have, I hope, shown
that Wagner was not the rhetorician always; that he could
engage in superb yieldings, in acts of grace to small things.
David has his ecstasy as triumphant as any large-spanned

crescendo of Siegfried when suddenly he realizes, as he sings *his* trial song to his master, that Johannisfest is the nameday also of Hans Sachs. 'Hans! Hans! Hans! Herr Meister, 's ist eu'r Namenstag.' And he gives his master a sausage.

V

In his art as in his life Wagner took appalling risks. The whole point of the plot-interest of *Meistersinger* is that Walther will sooner or later sing a great melody, a Preis-lied. The Preislied, in fact, is the hero of the opera. Now I do not confidently assert that the Preislied, composed not by Walther and Sachs but by Wagner, is a great melody beyond all argument. Eric Blom has stated in print that it is an atrocious melody. Sometimes I think that Beckmesser's serenade in Act II is a more cunningly made tune, and more distinguished, despite the false accents. But the point is that Wagner staked the fate of his work on his ability to compose a melody which would convince the majority of his listeners, all over the world and in different ages, that it *was* a Preislied, nothing more nor less. He wrote the melody demanded by the situation and the occasion, a melody which at the same time could be used simply as one strand in the variegated tissue of the score as a whole, would glorify Walther and also have in its phrases some tone or cadence fit to serve Hans Sachs when in the quintet he sings of his secret sadness ('Vor dem Kinde lieblich hehr, Mocht' ich gern wohl singen'). In *Meistersinger* Wagner gambled with the theories of a lifetime, played fast and loose with his own aesthetic of opera, and reverted to traditional ideas, with aria, concerted pieces, even a waltz. Wagner, the author of *Oper und Drama*, the apriorist in a thousand letters and essays, was really the instinctive musician, top and bottom. After he had composed *Tristan* he wrote of it

D   49

that it was the fulfilment in excelsis of his ideas. This was his theory of opera objectified. Then from the new world of chromatics discovered by Wagner in *Tristan* he, as we have seen, voyaged to a world of diatonics. Where is the modern composer capable of breaking free from his particular system at the prompting of imagination? Suppose a Schönberg were visited by a musical idea or feeling which demanded to be expressed diatonically; could he fit such an idea into the atonal system? Wagner, of course, did not say to himself before he composed *Tristan* and *Meistersinger*: 'Ah, now I must use a chromatic harmony for this work. But for my next, obviously I must "react" against chromaticism and employ mainly diatonics.' That is the contemporary way of making music. Tragedy by its intensity mixed the chromatic colours of Wagner's palette; comedy, broad and spacious, mixed the bright colours of the bannered music that is *Meistersinger*.

I know of no instance amongst the voluminous writings of Wagner where he discusses his own technique, and takes us into his musical workshop. On most other subjects, how to do this or that, physical, metaphysical, animal, vegetable, mineral; from the world as Will and Representation to Vegetarianism; from Greek tragedy to alliteration in verse; from anti-Semitism to Vivisection – on all things under the sun does he seek to enlighten us, except on his own method of composing. He left us mountains of self-explanation of Wagner the philosopher; Wagner the poet; Wagner the political theorist; Wagner the critic; Wagner the complete 'ologist, in fact. He expounded other composers; his essay on Beethoven is a masterpiece of interpretation. Upon the important question of the *How* of his own music he gives us scarcely a word of illumination; he tells us endlessly what it means but seldom does he give us a peep into his technical workshop. He wrote volumes about the nature of music in

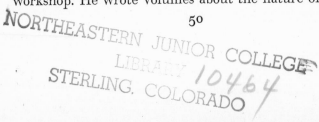

the abstract, about the relation of music to drama. Artists as a rule do not write critical accounts of themselves; and if Wagner had not spread his pen analytically in so many directions I should no more be astonished at his silence on his methods of composition than I am astonished at the silence of, say, Brahms about *his* methods and technique. Apparently Wagner thought that his music did not need discussion; he took it for granted. A man writes about his philosophy of life; about his economic and political theories; about marriage, death, divorce and bimetallism, but he does not think for a moment of writing about his breathing apparatus. Wagner took music in his stride while he strode all the cultural ways of the world and at the same time lived prodigiously. There is a letter somewhere amongst his published correspondence in which he relates to a friend that he has almost completed a music-drama: 'I wrote the final words of the libretto yesterday; I have now only the music to compose.' The point of this remarkable observation is that music was implicit in a Wagner libretto while he was committing it line by line to paper. It is a delusion – and one which Wagner seemed at times himself to share – that he first wrote a libretto and then by a separate and different creative art composed the music, fitting it in to words, to the incidents, emotional plan and sequence of a text conceived independently. Every sentence in a Wagner libretto was as a vein of music waiting to flow as soon as opened.

I have discussed the fact that a Wagner libretto contains a shape and design essentially musical. Examine a Wagner libretto and you will see at once that the various episodes are frequently grouped in a way that suggests a musical and not a dramatic ground-plan, sometimes observing even the hallowed A-B-A division. At the beginning of *Tristan*, for example, the steersman sings his melody; then comes the scene between Isolde and Brangäne; and after the climax, where Isolde calls for air ('Luft! Luft!'), we hear the steersman's song again. In the libretto this repetition marks a new scene but musically it is nothing but a subtly transformed ritornello. The reader will find many other instances throughout the libretti of *Tristan* and the 'Ring' to support the argument that Wagner conceived his text primarily as a musician. Certain it is that he seldom in his mature works followed his own theory, which was to make music the means and not the end, the servant and not the master. No librettist who attended primarily to dramatic requirements would recall, as Wagner constantly does, an emotional *point d'appui*. He himself described music as an art of transition; thus in a phrase he put the main problem of the composer – how to endow music with continuous vitality, a form really organic and not artificially supported by outmoded devices left over from sonata-form, or bridge-passages thrown over different sections like ladders, or double-bars, helpful and restful as milestones on the high-way but as arbitrarily planted there and as little connected with the growth and shape of the whole. The ideal of form in any art is described in a famous passage by Coleridge which Newman often quotes with affection and point: 'Shakespeare's intellectual action is wholly unlike that of Ben Jonson or Beaumont and Fletcher. The latter see the totality of the sentence or passage, and then project it entire. Shakespeare goes on creating and evolving B out of A, C out of B, and so on, just as a serpent moves, which makes a fulcrum of its own body, and seems for ever twisting and untwisting its own strength.' Makes a fulcrum of its own body – this is exactly what the music, or rather the orches-tra, of Wagner does. I have suggested that Wagner often elaborates the A-B-A ground-plan, that he even returns to a main subject (using the word 'subject' with not only musical but psychological and dramatic connotations). For another example of this strictly musical procedure, examine the curve of the scene in Act II of *Tristan*, from the Prelude beginning with the sounding of the 'Day' motif to the extinguishing of the torch and the coming of Tristan. Here is the most cunning movement onward by the fulcrum process, by the evolution of B out of A, and C out of B; then when the arch is traversed we return to a point of rest, a base, which as soon as we reach it is immediately changed to a new starting-point. The first bars of the Prelude to Act II of *Tristan*, the 'Day' motif, propel the music into life and motion; we next hear the 'subsidiary' themes (subsidiary in the sense that Othello and Desdemona and Iago are 'subsidiary' to the play's main and dominant theme of jealousy). These subsidiary themes are the rising figure of Isolde's impatience; Isolde's ardour; the horns of the night-hunt. The working out of these motifs is entirely symphonic, and when we reach Isolde's cry, 'Dein Werk, O tör'ge Magd', development and recapitulation are intermingled, until at the climax, 'lachend sie zu löschen zag' ich nicht', the 'Day' motif is sounded in tragic transformation, and now the music turns on itself again to the theme of the ardour of Isolde, and to the tense, interrupted, expectant phrases heard immediately after the first announcement of the 'Day' motif at the beginning of the prelude to this act.

As I say, the reader will find endless instances in Wagner of this organic musical movement onward, growth from the inside, with a constant renewal from basic seeds; all Wagner's returnings to a given subject are like a fresh fertilization of the soil. I do not claim that Wagner is nowhere reduced to shifts and paddings; the worlds of the music-dramas were too vast to encompass unaided by one or two mechanically built bridges. But taking a large view of his work we can usually find an organic form, thoroughly musical, compared with which the form of most other composers is mere joinery and carpentry – they are as woodworkers engaged on sectional bookcases, while the Wagnerian tree grows from a primary seminal energy to the topmost branch.

VI

It is the oddest irony that Wagner, one of the closest of thinkers in music, a composer of the strictest and most consecutive musical logic, a composer so fundamentally musical that his libretti were conceived in terms of balanced musical periods and patterns – this is the composer who is discussed most times in extra-musical language; indeed, is often discussed as though he had written only the words of his music-dramas and his various pamphlets and what not, and left us no music at all. He was himself, of course, much to blame for the mass of verbiage under which his immediate posterity has half buried him. Through the clouds and mists of his expositions and interpretations and theorizings it needs clear-sighted and unprejudiced vision to distinguish the musical wood from the polemical trees. So wide was the range covered by Wagner in his determination to set the world right once and for all, that it is possible to prove from his written work, from his endless spate of words, words, words, that he was the upholder of everything under the sun. Inevitably the germs of Nazism have been discerned in the 'Ring', though I have still to be instructed exactly at what part of the trilogy the monster raises his head. Wagner did not turn to the pagan myths for inspiration from any prophetic sense of the imminence of a new Nordic ideology. Only a profound ignorance of Wagner's aesthetic of opera could give credence to such an opinion. Wagner turned to myths because he realized that for his particular musical needs a libretto must deal with the type, not the individual; he instinctively knew that his style of music would not keep pace with a libretto which was marked with the tempo of contemporary life, or even of life in any dynamic epoch of history close enough to us to reveal a network of circumstance.[1]

I have been unable to obtain enlightenment as to whether Nazism was supposed to be symbolized by Siegfried or by Wotan; the adherents of the idea that the 'Ring' contains the Nazi credo seem lacking in unanimity on the point. For my own part I suggest that Alberich might stand for Hitler. But seeing that everybody and everything in the 'Ring' suffer a bad end, where does the Nazism of Wagner really come in? Bernard Shaw found in the 'Ring' an ideology far removed from Nazism; in *The Perfect Wagnerite* he explains Wagner in terms of socialism, the socialism of the 'nineties moreover. The Tarnhelm is the capitalist's tall hat which can lend a show of respectability to the profiteer. Fafner is the stupid wealth-worshipper sitting miserably on his money-bags, a slave to them. Wagner, social democrat in one age, Shaw regarding the music-dramas of the 'Ring' almost as the Fabian essays done into music! And then, in the 1940s, Wagner the mouthpiece of Hitler and the New Order! Well, well. Wagner told Judith Gautier that he was entirely without patriotism. The 'New' Reich of his day, he said, answered only in terms of the barest and most official orthodoxy. Germany did not understand that Shakespeare was worth more to England than all her colonies. He distrusted the Pan-Germanism of Bismarck.... All of these matters are irrelevant to our consideration of Wagner the artist; he could have been as Nazi as Hitler; or as anti-Nazi as Stalin, and his music would not have been affected; any political creed, any idea or ism,

[1] See *Oper und Drama*.

suffered a sea-change into something rich and strange as soon as it entered the mind of Wagner. Let us return to him.

It is not more stupid to say that *Meistersinger* and the 'Ring' is Nazi music than it is to say that *Tristan* is neurotic. Yet many intelligent musicians who admit the greatness of *Meistersinger* go to *Tristan* with a certain uneasiness of moral (or shall we say hygienic) conscience. Most of these people are, I am afraid, English. I do not know in what way a musical sound can be 'erotic'; in any case, an artistic expression of eroticism and a crude manifestation of eroticism are not the same thing. Art is, I gather, a catharsis. Tragedy of sex, or comedy of sex – in both instances we are taken by imagination beyond the trivial and the vulgar. I might not wish to meet the Herr Baron Ochs in real life; in Strauss's music he is not without his fascinations and genius. Let us suppose, for the sake of argument, that *Tristan* has its 'erotic' aspects. How could Wagner have treated a tragedy of love and passion without giving us certain erotic implications? Eroticism, my Oxford Dictionary tells me, denotes sex. Is it suggested that Wagner should have composed 'pure' music for Tristan and Isolde, music akin to that of Pamina and Pamino? I have only to ask the question to reveal its absurdity. Besides, the fact is that *Tristan und Isolde* gives us not only one aspect of love in the greatest exaltation of love in all art outside Shakespeare. Wagner shows us not only the lover and his beloved, the 'erotic' aspect of this theme. He shows us most of the aspects of love: the selfless devotion of woman to woman, of faithful waiting-girl to her queen. Brangäne's love for Isolde is not less poignantly treated by Wagner than the love of the romantic protagonists. More moving still is the expression of devotion of man to man, the devotion of Kurwenal to his master. Where in the range of the arts is there anything much finer, sweeter, nobler and more embracing in its humanity than Wagner's picture (told in music, remember, as much as in words) of Kurwenal in Act III of this music-drama? Kurwenal patiently tending his dying knight, endeavouring in his own doglike way to understand a tragic ecstasy and woe which are far beyond the homely world of *his* experience; Tristan lifts himself up on his fever-ridden pallet and cries out of his heart: 'O Treue! hehre, holde Treue! Mein Kurwenal, du trauter Freund!' The cry is as melting in its pathos as the great cry of Isolde as she leans over the deathbed of her lover: 'Nur einmal, ach, nur einmal noch!' We have to turn to *Antony and Cleopatra* for the like of this wounding beauty, to 'Downy windows close', and to 'Give me my robe; put on my crown'. No performance of *Tristan* can be truthful to Wagner if Kurwenal and Brangäne are not as consummately played as Tristan and Isolde themselves. *Tristan* tells us in music once and for all of romantic love, passionate love, selfish love, love that considers the world well lost. Also it tells us of the love that serves and sacrifices, that suffers and waits, that dies in service and dies happy in service. This 'erotic' opera, indeed like all great works of art, possesses a fundamental ethic and a fundamental metaphysic. The main and shattering beauty of it all comes from the fact that Wagner set passion and ecstasy and pathos against a background of doom; the joys of the lovers are snatched briefly from a world in which even the inimical forces are not so much cruel as laden with sadness and fate. When Brangäne's voice calls from the watch-tower, 'Habet acht!' the menace goes beyond the immediate plot-interest and action; this music is not only expressing an incident in the drama, is not only expressing the voice and emotions of Brangäne as she warns the lovers that the night is passing and King Marke will soon return. Wagner constantly transcends the immediate needs of his theme. The watch-

tower music is dyed in rich bodeful colours; there is ardour
in the rising string sequences; the harp ravishes the score;
but the deep solemn fundamental harmonies sound the note
of mortality. The music evokes the sense of beauty perishable in a world where the sane active day has little use for
the obsessions of night. 'Tag und Tod mit gleichem
Streichen sollten uns're Lieb erreichen', sings Isolde; day
and death join in feud against excess of love and beauty.
We may argue in strict *a priori* logic that the second act of
Tristan is Schopenhauer changed to music; or, to be precise,
it is music composed by a mind deeply under the influence
of Schopenhauer. Mathilde Wesendonck no doubt warmed
the romantic and poetic impulse; but the metaphysic of
Schopenhauer is the opera's very element and air and
firmament and endless sea. The ecstasies and passions of the
lovers are but as rainbow gleams thrown for a moment
across the austere sky of a will-less, self-less universe. 'In
the folds of the dark banner that casts its shadow over
Tristan', wrote Wagner to Liszt, 'I shall enshroud myself.'
As I write these lines, a memory returns to me of a performance of *Tristan* at Salzburg years ago; the stage for the
closing scene and the 'Liebestod' was for once in a way not
flat and static, like a series of tableaux vivants. King Marke
looked down from a high wall of rock; a soft amber glow
seemed to burn around the dead Tristan and the trans-
figured Isolde, a visible symbol of the funeral pyre that
burned in the orchestra. Then, as Isolde sang, 'To sink, to
die', the light went slowly out, leaving the stage in lonely
gloom, with the bowed still figure of King Marke just
discernible against the deepening sky.

King Marke is musically and dramatically as beneficially
endowed with genius and dignity of point of view as the
lovers. Most other opera composers or dramatists would have
left him merely a part of the eternal triangle. He is made

to represent the noblest aspect of love; wise understanding love that covers like a cloak. It is often argued that the appearance of Marke in Act II is anticlimax. In a drama without music, his long speech after the betrayal by Melot would certainly have tried the patience. But here is another proof of the essentially musical design behind Wagner's libretto sequence; after the climax of the duet between Tristan and Isolde, a point of rest was needed in the musical shape as well as in the psychological tempo. Moreover, Marke's music is here a supremely beautiful statement of his point of view; Wagner, who was so incapable in real life of seeing anybody's point of view except his own, was without prejudice or intolerance in his dealings with the people of his imagination. Marke's music is bowed with grief at Tristan's duplicity; not a note of jealousy is heard, no anger; the bass clarinet is the voice of sorrow, it asks the question before Marke opens his mouth:

> This to me, Tristan?
> Where now are truth and honour fled
> If Tristan all hath lost?

I can feel no lowering at all of the musical pulse in Marke's music; the artist who sings it is as well endowed as the others. Yet this music has been called tedious, is indeed still called tedious even by people who admire the opera on the whole. I invite the reader to look at the score and contemplate only two sections of Marke's address ('Mir dies? Dies, Tristan, mir?') at the words, 'die so herrlich hold erhaben mir die Seele musste laben'; and the closing phrases: 'Den unerforschlich tief geheimnisvollen Grund, wer macht der Welt ihn kund?' Not even Isolde, in the 'Liebestod', has more moving things to utter. And the player of the bass clarinet, if he has a soul at all, will not forget that here is a part for his instrument without an equal in eloquence; if orchestral music knows writing more expressive for bass clarinet than this, more appropriate to it, I should like to know where it may be studied.

There are only a few bars of meaningless fabricated music in the score of *Tristan* and it is all given to Melot. Here is another light on Wagner's psychological make-up. He has been called theatrical rather than musical, but he was not interested in Melot, who is merely a piece of machinery necessary to the stage action. Where is the opera composer other than Wagner who would have left Melot without a note of music to sing; would Verdi have resisted a temptation so strong – the Verdi who in recent years has been chosen as a centre from which to react against the rhetoric of Wagner? Melot was needed for the plot-interest; *somebody* had to expose Tristan to Marke. But Melot had nothing in him of what Wagner called the stuff of music. So he remains a lay figure in a score which breathes life and tragic significance and the quality of lovableness even into the Shepherd in his few bars of recitative, not to mention the great cor-anglais melody which is supposed to be the Shepherd's own composition as he watches for Isolde's ship. Melot is a stray from a prosaic world – poverty-stricken in the midst of romantic plenty, because he did not invade the mind of Wagner to its musical interior, but remained on the periphery, where Wagner the librettist occupied himself with plots and stratagems and potions and the general machinery of circumstance.

VII

On Christmas Day 1870, the 'Siegfried' Idyll was played on the staircase of Wagner's home in Switzerland; the music wakened Cosima on the morning of her thirty-third birthday. Everybody knows the story of how the Triebschen serenade came romantically into being. But a most significant fact seems to have eluded the attention even of the legioned army of Wagner commentators; the 'Siegfried' Idyll is the one and only work composed by Wagner without a preliminary discussion on his part; without an essay or pamphlet by him on its significance, without an explanatory reading or a communication to his friends, assembled to be talked at or lectured for hours. Wagner, before beginning to compose the music of all his major works, elaborated by pen or word of mouth the aesthetic or ethical or philosophical principles underlying them. The 'Siegfried' Idyll was written furtively; it was kept a dead secret in the villa at Triebschen. For weeks Wagner worked on it, and whenever Cosima walked into his study he would hastily hide the score in a drawer. He was at the time moulding the mighty coping stone of *Götterdämmerung*; he composed the 'Idyll' in his spare time, so to say, tossed it off much as Andrea del Sarto might have tossed off a Christmas card in moments of rest while painting masterpieces for the four walls of heaven. The point I wish to stress is that the 'Siegfried' Idyll is the only work of the mature Wagner that was conceived for music's sake – with love of Cosima the occasion. This work has not to fit in with a lifetime's theories about the Zukunftsmusik; in other words, as soon as Wagner found himself free for a moment to compose without responsibility to his aesthetic, he composed his only fine example of absolute music. This important fact obtains an even more intriguing interest when we recollect that in the last years of his life Wagner contemplated writing a symphony. We are able to infer from the 'Siegfried' Idyll what form this symphony would have taken: the fulcrum method of continuous movement, with the end seen in the beginning, and all the parts growing and emerging from one another, B out of A, C out of B; no artificial divisions;

61

no waiting for a change of gear, for a change of the red light to green at a crossroad in the music's onward course; no waiting even for the amber light signifying a point of rest and a new point of departure. The symphony which died unborn in Wagner might well have truly fulfilled his principle of music as an art of transition. So we come to the great irony of his life. He was *au fond* musician. But he followed Beethoven, and it was necessary that somebody should complete Beethoven's work – the fertilization of music by drama. Beethoven found music mainly an objective art, an art of patterned tone. Through eighteenth-century forms of instrumental music, Mozart marvellously drew *his* men and women: Don Giovanni, Donna Anna, Leporello, Susanna, the Countess, and the Queen of the Night. The formal limitations of the music of his period kept Mozart's genius within the ordered scope of comedy; the shadows were thrown from his temperament; tragedy crept in, to echo Dr Johnson's remark. He transcended a medium which not yet had been drenched in the dyes of mortality. With a few chords, two or three simple inversions, Mozart created Sarastro, true; but the sublime style had been implicit in music from the beginning. Beethoven stirred music with the sense of pity and heroic frustration; Dionysius succeeded unto Apollo, or rather Beethoven recreated music after the image of Prometheus. None the less, he left music still in the empyrean of the sublime. There is no sex in Beethoven; his world is governed by an ethic; Leonora, in his only opera, is not a woman so much as a symbol of the 'Ewig-Weibliche'.

To ravish the fair body and mind of music the fates chose Wagner. He steeped the art in humanity; he taught it love sacred and profane, acquainted it with good and evil. Like his own Wanderer he came down to earth and polluted the godhead of absolute music to beget human children.

III
Brahms
1833-1897

Brahms

If I were compelled immediately to go and live for years on the desert isle of which so much has been heard, and if I were allowed to take with me only one composer, I think it would be Brahms. He might not satisfy all my moods, but he would attend to most of them. Other composers have risen higher than Brahms in a single direction; few have equalled him for range of musical interest and as a satisfying companion day by day for Everyman in all his humours. Then, again, Brahms is the composer for the middle-aged; there is in him that sanity and gently sedentary introspection which are the mark and haven of men who have recently emerged from the flowing tide and find themselves high, if not quite dry, on the maturing shore and sands. In Brahms we live again without excitement. He awakens memory, not desire; he gathers the harvest of romance rather than sows the seeds – which most of all renders him the aptest company for us on our desert island where, I take it, passion will be best recollected in tranquillity.

Brahms achieved a masterpiece in nearly every form of music; one exception was opera – and as on desert islands the chances of hearing opera are likely to be as rare as in all the by no means deserted islands of the British Empire, away from London, we shall not on one account wish we had brought some other composer with us instead of Johannes. He will not appeal to the forward-reaching mind, maybe – if in these days any being in the prime of his faculties would wish to indulge in what we once confidently

E

65

called progress. Here again, though, Brahms would suffer no shortcomings as our one and only source of music on an uncharted coral strand; we may all become our own atonalists whenever we will. If we should wish to hear chamber music, there is a masterpiece by Brahms in most of the known instrumental combinations, including one or two without peer: the Clarinet Quintet, for instance. The Violin Concerto is one of the few works which no fiddler dare leave alone if he would convince the world of his rank. The three violin sonatas of Brahms have not been surpassed for variety of style and rich and happy marriage of the two instruments. In the Opp. 116, 117, 118, Brahms contributed to the literature of the piano as importantly and as originally as Schumann, to say the least. The vocalist who ignored the world of the Brahms Lieder would expose both his ignorance and poverty; here our composer is with Schubert, Wolf and Schumann, if he is not as great as two of these as a maker of German song. His four symphonies have been accepted by the majority of cultured and experienced musicians throughout the world and over a long period as amongst the permanent peaks in the great range of symphonic music. The pianist who wishes to satisfy us that he is built in the big mould must sooner or later face the challenge of the two concertos of Brahms. In variation-form, Brahms has not been excelled for fancifulness and ripeness of technique. He will feed middle-aged philosophy with his 'Vier Ernste Gesänge', and his 'Requiem' and 'Alto Rhapsody', just as readily as in the 'Liebeslieder' waltzes he will compel an avuncular *Rückblick* on old delights long since packed away in the lavender cupboard of our days. Brahms wrote as little insignificant music as anybody who, having been tenanted by genius, was obliged to write a good deal. I hold to the opinion that only the small and second-rate artist is meagre of output. Brahms

66

destroyed many of his works, so critical was he of his own efforts; yet he left behind a body of composition which if we should be unable to escape from, or if we should prefer to remain on our desert island for ever, would keep us in touch with the art in most of its vital aspects; indeed Brahms provides us with a very anatomy of Music, and at the same time breathes into it the breath of a full man who worked in a rich field and period.

II

In the strange history of the life and survival of critical opinions the music of Brahms occupies an ironical chapter. Most writers on music must at nights see passing before them a dreadful array of pitiful ghosts of statements and judgments once born of vigorous pens and sent belligerently kicking into the world; now they pass in hideous cavalcade, like the midnight review before Richard III. When I was a boy, Brahms was accepted as the last word in classical complexity and profundity; not only had he been hailed by Hans von Bülow as one of the 'three Bs' of music; none other than Ernest Newman had written of the 'colossal intellect' functioning behind the B flat Piano Concerto; and he, the same Mr Newman – who now would scarcely praise Brahms for fundamental brainwork – quoted with approval Sir Hubert Parry's fantastical description of the Variations on a Theme of Haydn – 'His [Brahms's] principles are in the main those of Beethoven, while he applies such devices as condensation of groups of chords, anticipations, inversions, analogues, sophistications by means of chromatic passing notes, etc.' (that 'etc.' is good), 'with an elaborate but fluent ingenuity which sometimes makes the tracing of a theme in a variation quite a difficult intellectual exercise.'

Mr Newman went on to state that Brahms's 'aloofness from other men', 'his austerity' were never more clearly shown than in the 'St Antoni' Variations.

I remember reading these forbidding remarks of Sir Hubert and Newman in an analytical note of a programme of a Hallé concert in Manchester, which I attended when I was very young. Newman was then the music-critic of the *Manchester Guardian*: and what he said or wrote was accepted by all of us (or nearly all) as holy writ. I also remember the guilty feeling which came over me, after I had worked myself up into the state of cerebration deemed suitable by these two mentors for a proper appreciation of the 'St Antoni' Variations: so far from finding anything intellectual about the music, I blasphemously enjoyed the entrancing rhythm, the gracious melody, the sturdy elbowing movement onward; and at last the golden opening out of the finale, burgeoning as a sunrise on a full sea. I was not a precocious boy, and not at all schooled in composition. Next day I spoke of my enjoyment of Brahms to Dr Brodsky, who at the time was principal of the College of Music in Manchester; Brodsky had long ago known Brahms, and had played the Violin Concerto with the composer conducting. Even Brodsky seemed a little taken aback that a novice should have found Brahms so easy: 'You should *admire* Brahms, my boy,' he said; 'but not already is it that you can enjoy him.' I suppose that I, like other young folk of my own age in those days, had not been scientifically prepared for the right approach to Brahms. I knew only of the thrill I experienced whenever I heard 'Wie bist du, meine Königin'; I knew only of the wave of happiness that flooded me whenever I heard the beginning of the A major Violin Sonata and the piano played its first solo chorded song, with its extended and rocking arpeggios; I knew only of the rapt spell that seemed to hold me in suspense as the music of 'Feldeinsamkeit' spun its magic of noonday heat and quietude. I knew only of the twilight grove of the second movement of the Violin Concerto; and when I heard Elena Gerhardt sing 'Das Mädchen spricht' I was almost forced to the conclusion that there must be two Brahms and that I had been listening to the wrong and inferior, because melodious, one. And so persistently do first lessons and ideas tyrannize, so difficult is it to fight against established judgments, that though early in life I found myself on the true track of Brahms the romantic and humanist, not until many years passed by was I able to penetrate the gloom in which the D minor Piano Concerto had been enveloped; then I discovered that even here was a warmth and graciousness of song and harmony which, once in the heart, stays there for good and all. Brahms was himself responsible no doubt for the unfriendly first aspect put forth by this concerto. The first movement, originally intended as a symphonic first movement expressing sorrow at the news of Schumann's attempted suicide, is for a while the music of impotence; it takes its birth from a chilly pit of orchestration. Brahms writes low-pitched notes for nearly all the instruments; we feel that not yet has he learned to understand how to write for them. But after the piano has played the second subject, and we have heard it taken up by the strings with the most gorgeous decorations by the piano, then we know – or we should know – that Brahms has expelled grief from his concerto. It is, in fact, one of the most genial concertos of all in its quick movements; and the slow movement reveals Brahms at his most lovably tender and reflective – and as an artist in the orchestral diminuendo.

Today the legend of the austerity of Brahms is passing; and another is taking its place, as different and as misleading. The latest legend would persuade us that Brahms, so far from having possessed an intellect capable of grasping

large musical forms, was really incapable of composing at all
in bulk, but was a miniaturist, a meanderer, reduced to all
sorts of reach-me-down shifts in his development-sections –
a sort of cobbler of the symphony. In an essay on Sibelius,
Mr Newman quotes with a show of approval Wagner's
opinion that much of Brahms is 'mere note-spinning, according to rule, a mere filling-in of a conventional mould, the
mere elaboration of a transmitted pattern'. Brahms, like one
or two other composers, was at times compelled to eke out
a symphonic development-section by reach-me-down formulae. But this kind of patchwork would not necessarily
have been avoided by rejection of a 'transmitted pattern'.
I do not quite see how any great artist, with something to
say, can altogether neglect transmitted patterns or forms.
Mr Newman himself has argued in his book, *A Music
Critic's Holiday*, that 'one of the laws of progress in music
seems to be that it comes about, at first, largely through the
activity of men of the second rank; the men of the first rank
have, in the first place, a great deal to express, and in the
second place know instinctively that it can be expressed only
in a language that is already, as the result of long evolution, copious and flexible'. Again: 'In our own day any
musician of intelligence would shrink from the task of
trying to make a completely new symphonic structure of
the size and scope of the old; he would know that to build
on that scale one has to take over, in music as in architecture, the accumulated knowledge and skill and much of the
material of preceding generations.' True. Very true. Mr
Pecksniff was sensible, when, by adding a doorstep, he made
Martin Chuzzlewit's grammar school his own; suppose he
had not started from a transmitted pattern? He would not
have got as far as the doorstep. When in a symphonic
passage Brahms is reduced to padding or to mechanical
exploitation of scholarship; when his music is too obviously

durchkomponiert, we need not drag in 'transmitted patterns' to account for the trouble; a momentary weakening of inspiration will explain everything.

In recent years criticism has tended too much to consider music in terms of form, or as the cant phrase has it, 'physiology'. The reaction against romanticism has been responsible for the fact that nowadays critics are afraid of emotional connotations in their writings. They discuss a musical score as though it were an architect's blueprint; they affect to devote more attention to the ground-plan of the symphonic edifice than to the spirit dwelling therein. Music, we are bidden, must be listened to *qua* music; that is, without 'extraneous' ideas or impressions in our minds – which is the equivalent to telling the young lover that he should look at the starlit sky *qua* astronomy, or at his beloved *qua* anatomy. The first attribute of genius is, as Arnold Bennett writes somewhere, 'fineness of mind'. Above all, 'the artist's mind must be permeated and controlled by common sense. But he must be able to conceive the ideal without losing sight of the fact that it is a human world we live in, and his mind must have the quality of being noble'. Bennett might well have been describing Brahms; for if ever a composer was noble, humane and permeated and controlled with common sense, it was Brahms. Granted that here and there he succumbed to the temptation to compose a bridge-passage by the book of arithmetic, does anybody suggest that he for a moment expressed or gave evidence of indolence, lack of the artist's conscience or meanness or any smallness whatever? Form in music, I repeat, cannot be considered in the abstract; form in music is expression. No composer has so far solved the problem of a form and sequence of music which shall develop with each and every note or phrase born of each and every preceding note or phrase, a form containing no lacunae, a form which is

forgetive (in Falstaff's term) in every part, and every part
essential to the vitality of the others. Music, unlike the
sister arts, must live much on itself; it is the divine spider.
The poet and painter and novelist can turn to life and the
external universe for substance and shape; even the poet,
who approaches nearest to the composer's 'Intense inane'[1]
is free, whenever rhythm and 'pure poetry' are failing him,
to draw on the support of the association-value of words.
Music must weave its golden ladder strand by strand; the
composer, in fact, is the Indian rope-climber of the arts;
Brahms was not one of the lightweights amongst composers,
so it was inevitable that from time to time he should come
down to earth with a bump.

Nearly every instance in Brahms of an excrescence in the
shape of a superfluous convention that gets in the way can
be explained in terms of the nature of the materials of
symphonic music as they existed when Brahms began to
work in them. It is not generally realized that Brahms was
the first composer to achieve a synthesis of the classical
and romantic styles; he was the offspring of Beethoven and
Schubert. In Brahms the Lied has grown up to a symphony;
also, the classical instrumental patterns or forms are
enriched by romantic melody and cadence. Brahms restored
to music the ethic and heroic austerity from which it turned
or withdrew during the first flush of the romantic movement; and to the single-minded heroic and moral tone of
Beethoven, Brahms lent the impulse of lyrical feeling. He
matured romance by a classical seriousness of mind; and to
song he added the classical instrumental technique. The
formal weaknesses in Brahms – and they have been grossly
exaggerated – sprang from a clash of the two styles, freshly
mated. In places we feel that Brahms is clogging the

---

[1] I had better point out that I use 'inane' in the Matthew Arnold–Shelley
sense, denoting a void, with no 'silly' connotation whatever.

romantic impulse by a conscientious design derived from the traditional patterns; in other places we feel that the romantic impulse is taking too modest, easy and narrow a course to fill the varied and spacious classical channels. The chamber music of Brahms reveals a number of examples of the classic imposing his will and knowledge on the reluctant romantic; and in the third movement of the Third Symphony there is an obvious case of a symphonic tailor patching a pretty folk-song garment with material taken from the gown of the scholar. These lapses from a firm natural binding together of the classical and romantic sheaves were inevitable. As I say, they were inherent in the materials Brahms harvested; but they count for so little amongst his bounty that we are at liberty to emulate the Scottish preacher who said: 'And now, brethren, we come to a deeficult passage, and having looked it boldly in the face, we will pass on.' I do not believe that Brahms 'boldly passed on' more difficulties in symphonic logic than other masters of music, whose 'continuous logic' is quoted to us so frequently as a model. The wonder is that in building the bridge from classicism to a mature romanticism he used as few props and stays as he did. It is certainly odd that the high priests of Wagnerism have preferred Bruckner as a symphonist to Brahms – the same Wagnerites who swear by the Master's theory of music as an art of transition, a continuous web of tone unfolded from its own inner loom. There is, of course, no continuous tissue at all in Bruckner's music, no subtlety of transition. Bruckner when he comes to the end of an episode simply pauses, then begins again. You can see him pulling out a new stop on his organ of an orchestra. There are noble ideas in Bruckner and little inner and inevitable growth. But he sometimes used the Wagner tubas; that apparently was enough to render him liable to more or less military service in the great war against Brahms – poor Anton who loved God, and never wished to offend the smallest of his creatures.

The problem of symphonic form cannot be solved *a priori*; each artist must and will find his own way. I cannot agree with Mr Newman that this problem in the main is one of an 'insensible merging of one bar into another throughout the entire work'. The one-movement-continuous-tissue symphony will no doubt suit and satisfy one type of creative musical mind; others will as certainly prefer the stronger contrasts of the symphony in two and more movements. It is not as certain as the Wagnerites seem to imagine that the music of the future will perpetually observe the method of imperceptible development; there are and always will be artists who revel in traditional forms or conventions for the sake of shaping or adapting them to a new material. There are even artists who, having looked the 'deeficulty' of a transmitted pattern boldly in the face, prefer not to pass it by but to enjoy a struggle with the intractable circumstances of their art. The poet is not reduced to impatience by the artificialities of the sonnet-form. I suggest it was not Brahms who, having looked the difficulties of symphonic form boldly in the face, passed them by; rather I submit that it is in the Seventh Symphony of Sibelius that we can find a 'classic' evasion of the problem at issue – how to compose a symphony which though it dispenses with the older divisions and compartments and repetitions and bridge-passages and so on, will none the less be at once recognized as a symphony. In the Seventh Symphony, Sibelius telescopes the divisions and reduces his material to a basic theme or two – not so much themes as nuclei of notes; in other words, he condenses symphonic syntax and logic. But as I point out in the chapter on Sibelius in this book, there are four movements to be discerned in the Seventh Symphony. Single-movement form and continuous tissue are achieved by

Sibelius at the cost of that freedom of expansion, with unity in variety, which is the mark of the symphonic style. If you talk to me of a symphony of constricted and taciturn and not expansive music, I shall understand you no more than if you talk of a constricted and taciturn and not expansive epic. The fact is, as I see it, that the quality or condition of the symphonic style does not depend on a form but on a mode of feeling. Just as the term epic does not nowadays necessarily mean a verse-form, so has the term symphonic come to have a broader than strictly musical significance. We are free to speak of a symphonic sunset; or of a symphonic novel – Tolstoy's *War and Peace* for example. The essence of a symphonic style is its gradual unhurried and inevitable expansion, a movement and growth from seeds that produce the tree. The 'Scottish' Symphony of Mendelssohn is not symphonic – James Joyce's *Ulysses*, for all its enormous size, is not symphonic; it does not expand; it merely analyses moments of time, isolated experiences. The quality of being symphonic does not of course depend on bulk or duration but on power – power that expands, achieves an arch, and contains its end in its beginning. But if the symphonic style does not depend on bulk and duration it certainly has nothing to do with economy and sparseness. I cannot imagine a small one-track-minded symphony. The symphonic style, in a word, is the man himself; if he has ampleness and richness and variety of mind and nature, then he is a symphonic man; and if he be a composer he will most certainly write symphonies, to whatever shape or design he inclines, new or old. If ever there was a symphonic man it was Johannes Brahms.

So far I have tried to define the style of Brahms, to show that he gathered in the crops of a sowing of Beethoven and Schubert, ripened to harvest by the warmth of his own genius. I have tried to relate him to the technical or stylistic (a hateful but convenient word) conditions in which he found the art of music, especially the *modus operandi* of symphonic development. I have tried especially to show that with Brahms, as with every other mortal artist, we should relate what we confidently call his 'faults' to the conditions and material of his art in his day: 'In der Beschränkung', says the wise Goethe, 'zeigt sich erst der Meister.'[1] A really scientific criticism would hesitate to use the word 'fault', as a description of some lesion or short-circuit in an artist's imaginative processes; better and more philosophical to call it a necessary trait of style. I am not of course referring to obvious crudities, such as the mannered chromaticism of a Spohr, or the hauled-up pulleys of a Puccini soprano and tenor unison climax. We are considering the so-called defects of the works of a recognized master. Can we think of any one of the masters except as we now know him, 'warts and all'? It was once affirmed that Brahms's orchestration was without colour and facility. Would his severest critic, knowing Brahms as he should know him – that is as so much human psychology, temperament, spirit, blood and sinew turned to music – would this critic have the orchestration of Brahms altered? The business of criticism is to root out the superfluities or irrelevances in an artist's style; fortunately most great artists attend to the job themselves, before the critic is called in at all. Critics might with a refreshing humility consider this point, especially when they are dealing with a composer as ruthlessly self-critical as Brahms. He was not an impulsive son of nature, like Schubert, whose music exposes sometimes many signs of hastiness which any fool can see. We might with profit here attend to Donald Tovey: 'If every one of Brahms's works in sonata-form rewards the effort of

[1] The master finds himself by observing the law, the limitations of his medium.

76

a reasoned defence on all points on which attack has been directed, this is not because Brahms is infallible, or acceptable only to those who are ready to take him as gospel. It is, on the contrary, because Brahms was so far from thinking himself infallible that he consented to the publication of nothing to which he had not devoted more severe criticism, long after the work was finished, than could be collected from all the sensible remarks that have been made on his works since they appeared.'[1]

When we come to think of it – and it is a conclusion to which the philosophy of years eventually leads us – genius must be taken as we find it. Can we possibly think of any genius except as he has incarnated himself in his works? If he is a genius his faults will be relevant and part of his constitution; maybe – a more searching thought – the 'fault' may be a necessary constituent in the whole, the dash of poison that retains good health. A phrase of Ethel Smyth comes to mind: let it be printed in warning letters before the desks of all critics: 'Where is the error, and can it be corrected without imperilling something essential?' And directly underneath Dame Ethel's awe-inspiring query let the phrase of Brahms himself be written: not in letters of fiery admonition but in good honest everyday calligraphy: 'Das sieht jeder Narr!'

III

It is proved already that Brahms is little better than one of the great geniuses of music; and it will go near to be thought so shortly. Thus may Dogberry the critic speak now. I am not, of course, suggesting that we should bow down without question or doubt before the masters; proper appreciation of a work of art depends as much on a

[1] Essay on Brahms in Cobbett's *Survey of Chamber Music.*

perception of its limitations as of the fully realized parts. We must look out for features of style that do not belong to the composer; the only 'faults' that matter are irrelevances; nobody is privileged to point out to genius any other sort of 'fault'. It is not enough to say that Brahms sometimes expresses impotence, as in sections of the first movement of the C minor Symphony; he may have wished to express impotence; an easy confident style in this movement would have been the worst of all artists' faults – which is to talk beside the subject. The dichotomy of classical and romantic characteristics of technique was not irrelevant, as we have seen, to the style of Brahms. If the elements do not always happily mingle, very well then; we are the readier to enjoy the marvellous hymeneal when they do. Let me once again stress the fact that Brahms was the first composer to bring the classical and romantic technique of expression to complete and fruitful union; it was an amazing marriage. Beethoven had fertilized the symphonic soil for any seed of expression; from Schubert's untidy but lovely garden seeds were blown over the years to Brahms's field, where he tilled with implements forged in the same foundry which forged Beethoven's. Schubert's gorgeous plant blew to falling leaves and petals too soon in the C major Symphony, for want of a deep-rooted symphonic-trunk. Brahms grafted it on a stouter tree, which naturally acquired a knotty twisted branch here and there. Without the knots there could have been no stout trunk. It is because there is so much of breadth in Brahms, so many aspects of the man, that narrow folk are sure sooner or later to find him rubbing them the wrong way.

Suppose that on the desert island a castaway is washed up, and that he is a musician entirely different in mind and nature from myself; whether I like it or not he must be my only companion for goodness knows how long.

Well, though we shall certainly quarrel on many things –
two individuals day by day thrust into one another's way
would occasionally have to quarrel or die – we shall not
quarrel about music. For suppose that my companion is
anti-romantic, one of William James's tough-minded fraternity, and I the opposite, a lover of sentiment – moonshine, if
you like. Well, my companion need not listen (I take it that
a piano and a gramophone, with all extant records of Brahms,
has been saved from the wreck); he need not listen while
I am playing the first movement of the Second Symphony,
with its mysterious horns at the outset, and the darkening
forest of an orchestra, where solemn trombones seem to
loom before us – trees as men walking – and the low distant
thunder of drums is heard; he need not listen to the G
major Violin Sonata, need not come into its intimate world,
where fancy and gentle melancholy sing together, a
twilight piece, silver-greyness in everything. The rich glow
of the third movement's dark empurpled cloud would
doubtless offend his hard spirit; but he need not listen. Nor
need he even try for politeness' sake to share my rapture as
Brahms throws a rope of violin tone high to the turret of
the allegro of the Violin Concerto; likewise may he turn
away while I give myself to the Clarinet Quintet and the
solo instrument's gush of notes which fall on the evening
air like the song of Thomas Hardy's darkling thrush. Nor
need he be jealous of me as I sweeten my heart with the
'cello melody of the slow movement of the Second Piano
Concerto; or as I let my heart dance to the lilt of the waltzes;
or ripple my fingers in the gracious texture of the A major
Intermezzo; or as I leap down the hill of the opening of the
Third Symphony. No! my friend will not only not be
jealous; if there is another piano or gramophone handy he
may not even heed my enjoyment of Brahms the romantic;
he will be invigorating his mind with the gigantic

double-fugue of the piano variations on the Handel theme – a giant's causeway of a fugue; or he will scale the heights of the introduction to the C minor Symphony, with the Brahms who attempted to put himself by the side of Prometheus Beethoven and snatch fire from the gods; or he will revel in the daring and intricacy of the Paganini Variations – music which turns brains into fingers and fingers into brains. Or he will meditate on man's vanity as he listens to the 'Vier Ernste Gesänge'; or he will stimulate his intellect in the knotty rough weather of the finale of the Third Violin Sonata. He will go, too, with Brahms and Goethe into the questioning gloom of the 'Harzreise' – all these things our composer will feed him on. And the joke is that the laugh must always be on my side; for while he may not share my happiness in the romantic and lyrical Brahms, I shall share all the sterner delights of *his* choices. No; we should not quarrel about Brahms, my imaginary friend and I, in our desert isolation. And I can't think of any other composer who day by day could by himself likewise serve two dissimilar tastes in music and prevent contention and a sense of grievance on one side or the other.

There are, you see, surprises for all who come to Brahms for the first time after having heard of the legends still in circulation about him. I wish all young musicians whose minds hold echoes of the ancient chatter about the drabness and inhuman complexity of Brahms could have heard – and once heard, heard for a lifetime – a performance by Jelly d'Aranyi and the Hallé Orchestra of the Brahms Violin Concerto, conducted by Hamilton Harty at a Hallé concert years ago. A woman in the Brahms Violin Concerto? you might ask. People in the mid-nineteenth century certainly objected to a woman violinist in Brahms even as they objected to a woman composer of any music that didn't

sound like Chaminade. Brahms was regarded as entirely
masculine then – the twin B to Beethoven, born a little
later, but as hard of bone and no more concerned than
Beethoven with women in his music. There are no women
in Beethoven; at least none of marriageable years. Leonora
is really an abstract idea, an ideal, a musical sort of 'das
Ewig-Weibliche'. Nobody could make a ballad to *her*
eyebrow. But Brahms is often making love in his music,
no doubt in a middle-aged manner (as we have seen); but
many women like it that way. Is not the 'Sapphische Ode'
proof that Brahms did not inherit too much of the austerity
of Beethoven, who couldn't have written the song to save
his life? Well, the adagio of the Violin Concerto is not far
removed in spirit or tone from the 'Ode', though a touch of
the 'Wiegenlied' tenderness comes in to keep the music
close to the cradle in which so many slow movements of
Brahms are rocked. A notable fact about Brahms is that
many of his first subjects are strong and masculine and that
nearly all the second subjects are feminine.[1] That is perhaps
why his music is so rich and various: as Hans Sachs sings:

> Ob euch gelang
> Ein rechtes Paar zu finden
> Das zeigt sich jetzt zu Kinden.

Jelly d'Aranyi, niece of Joachim, revealed to me the
rarer glories of the Violin Concerto for the first time. When
the song of the second subject, with its full flowing sea of
braveness was reached, she rode on it gorgeously. And in
the adagio, where the fiddle never takes up the melody to
itself but muses upon the grave loveliness in some of the
most rapt decoration ever written, this highly spirited artist
played as one listening to half-heard sounds contained

[1] Consider first movements of the Third Symphony, the D minor Piano
Concerto, the Violin Concerto, etc.

F   81

within the wood of her own instrument. Then towards the close of this movement, where the rising curves of the violin and the quickening tempo suggest that beauty, having been rapt for so long, can no longer contain herself – then we saw Jelly d'Aranyi pressing her cheek to her violin as though giving warmth to it. And in the finale, she tossed back her head and flashed the vivacity of her nature into the Hungarian rhythms. I dwell on this memory, during a study of Brahms, not only for the pleasure recaptured, but because it is my main wish to present the Brahms that to this day is placed in the shadow of the more palpable giant. There is hardly a work by him – I do not exclude even the great Double Concerto – in which Brahms the intimate poet of mild-eyed romance may not be found. In this gritty work, and one or two more like it, the newcomer to the composer may well experience the delightful astonishment of the student of Browning, who having been warned of the obscurity and aridness of 'Sordello', one day comes across the lines which tell of Sordello and Palma, how they exchanged low laughter

> now would gush
> Word upon word, to meet a sudden flush.

As Brahms grew older he entwined more and more romantic garlands on the classical trellis. At times his mind seemed to develop in a direction contrary to that of most minds of men of genius. He did not, unlike Beethoven, for example, seek for a greater simplicity, a less and less sensuous tone; he did not become more and more elliptical in expression. He discovered a lyric vein and colour of which he apparently had little idea when he was a young man; that is, if he may be said ever to have been young. His early Piano Sonata in F sharp minor, composed before he was twenty, is a thousand years old in the head; and it is harsh and unfriendly; the rise of the legend of his austerity can be understood by an examination of most of the works of his youth and early manhood. Even his symphonies gain in the impulse of song as they succeed one another. In the C minor Symphony, Brahms made a magnificent effort to lift himself to the heroic austere heights of the greater Beethoven; but never again did he venture in that direction of sublime awe and loneliness. The Second and the Third are romantic symphonies; the Fourth is also lyrical *au fond*; the Passacaglia finale can be analysed in terms of rich enough melody. The C minor Symphony – fantastically hailed in its day as the Tenth – is glad to come down to the valleys, once the abyss of the first movement has been crossed. The allegretto has a miniature touch that would have gone in danger of its slender life in the smithy of music in which Beethoven forged his C minor Symphony, or the Ninth; the delicate texture of this allegretto might at any moment have been brutally torn by one of the hammer-blows which in Beethoven are constantly aimed at the heart of a movement. The main theme of the finale of the Brahms C minor Symphony, once on a time absurdly related in spirit to the main theme of the finale of Beethoven's Ninth, has, for all its breadth a certain ease and warmth of motion psychologically poles apart from Beethoven. It is almost a German drinking-song; it might easily have occurred during the 'Akademische-Fest' overture. The music of Brahms was seldom disturbed by the dramatic changeful stress which with Beethoven became the principal characteristic of the symphony. A contrast of Beethoven and Brahms in terms of orchestral dynamic will illumine this point. The art of music frequently seems unable to contain Beethoven; the drive of his daemon imperilled the whole symphonic structure; you can hear him shaking it with vast reiterated chords. We may realize how little inclined Brahms must have been to measure himself for the putting-on of Beethoven's mantle if we consider the frequency in Beethoven of reiterated notes and chords, and the comparative scarcity of them in Brahms. Forceful insistence on the same note or chord is a dramatic, not a lyrical device; it means a breaking-up of a song-sequence. Brahms's use of repeated-notes falls short of Beethoven's disregard of a melodic context; Brahms scarcely ever forgot that the reiterated chord is fatal to the flow and fullness of song. When Brahms's music does halt or contends gruffly, it does not forget the course of song; Brahms is merely clearing his throat and chest before beginning again. The reputation of Brahms as a man of austere mind and nature was largely the consequence of the need of the schools of his day; they insisted that he should carry the standard against the Wagnerians and Lisztians, especially the Lisztians and their so-called romanticism. The joke is that it was Brahms, not Liszt, who eventually came close to the heart of true romance. The romantic style in music runs to song; for it is a state or outcome of subjective emotion. The Lisztians sought to express in music the external event or character seen in an attitude. Their aim and effect were dramatic or pictorial; objective, in a word – certainly not romantic.

In Brahms youth looks ahead to age, and age finds another impulse, as wisdom glances back over the years. Hamburg joins hands with Vienna. Early spring frosts once threatened to freeze the flow of the melody of Brahms; but sunshine of high noon and maturity freed the source – and the source was never afterwards forgotten. It was, you may be surprised to realize, a folk-song source; it attained with its growing sweep and broadening banks a classic grandeur and dignity, yet it remained true, in its mildness and warmth, to its lowly origins. Schubert was the first composer of the bourgeoisie, but he did not live long enough to expel vagrancy from his art. In Brahms classicism and romanticism alike are fused in an urbane bloodstream; if at times the aspect of Brahms is a little uncompromising it is only on the surface. In his music, age approves of youth, as Samuel Langforth wrote, and both are bound together by the piety of consistent and noble art. And how various an art! Clearly he is the composer for our desert island; we have found the right man. We need only the desert island.

I V

Anton Bruckner
1824-1896

The Organ of St Florian

Anton Bruckner

In another part of this book I have called Bruckner and César Franck 'twin-souled', a good enough figure in its context but not entirely apt. The two composers lived and worked at the same time, but they really had little in common except devotion to the organ and religion. Bruckner was very much the peasant by nature; Franck can never be thought of as a peasant. Along with his Walloon blood went a conscious culture. He was not naive and unworldly in Bruckner's way. The chromatic melody of Franck lapses often into sentimentality or into the sensuous. In Bruckner there is no weak or lush chromaticism, no sentimentality, certainly little or no sensuousness. Architecturally, Franck may be related to the Gothic, Bruckner to the Baroque, though the influence on Bruckner of baroque ornament and baroque insistence on detail has been greatly exaggerated. Is it possible to think of a baroque mountain?

Franck at his prayers is not without awareness of himself; he strikes an attitude, ready for portrayal in stained glass. Bruckner is never aware of himself; he is lost to the world in worship. He does not supplicate. He is God-intoxicated. And it is a wholesome intoxication. No fumes, no incense. There is no awareness of evil in Bruckner's music, nothing daemonic. His Catholicism is Austrian and as likeable and humane as Haydn's. When Bruckner is not praising God from a grateful heart, he is enjoying nature. A Bruckner scherzo is genial, rustic, windswept. There is no fresh air in César Franck, no clodhopping yokels, no dreamy stretches of sunlit countryside. The two men were doubtless twin-souled in piety, but each wore his piety with a difference. Bruckner would probably have regarded César Franck as his superior socially and intellectually; and he would have been right. But Bruckner was the greater composer by far.

Bruckner's music is best approached by way of the Mass, which he used as a form of expression long before he composed the first of his symphonies. The Austrian *Landmesse* is devout and not terrorstricken, sublime by faith, never driven into it by fear of the devil. The duration and immense subdivisions in the outer and slow movements of a Bruckner symphony, the pauses, the beginnings-again, the fervent unisons – all these are features adapted from the Mass as Bruckner conceived and shaped it, influenced by memories in his ears of the organ resonance of St Florian.[1] He left his ninth and last symphony unfinished, the finale movement only sketched. It has become a custom to play the Bruckner Te Deum to round off performances of the Ninth Symphony; and the custom does no hurt to the mood and style of either. The Te Deum follows as naturally as if the symphony had suddenly but not unexpectedly broken into song, not a choiring of the cherubim but of an earthly aspiring strong-lunged company of vocal Bruckners. The main formal characteristics are much the same in all the truly representative Bruckner symphonies, especially in the Fifth, Sixth, Seventh, Eighth and Ninth. Four movements, and each of the four movements except the scherzo serious, annunciatory in diction, unhurrying in tempo.

In a Bruckner first or final movement an accumulation of imitated figures or insistent broken-chords in sequence is piled up to a gigantic fanfare ending as abruptly as a finale of the mature Sibelius, but in the case of Sibelius the end is

[1] He was organist in the chapel of the monastery of St Florian.

unexpected, while with Bruckner we have some time given up hope that the end will come at all. Bruckner's orchestra is like an organ and choir mingled, magnified and changed into instrumental tone. There is little psychological difference, little difference of content or expression, in one Bruckner symphony from another, though deepening and more subtle thought-processes govern the later ones. Bruckner was a single-minded composer; his theme or text is always much the same. His immense output took the shape of Mass or symphony; his solitary string quintet is a deviation from type, and occasionally strains the chamber medium hard. Though an accomplished organist, Bruckner wrote no solos for the instrument. Also he wrote nothing in variation-form. He conceived in terms of contrasts of tone, with polyphonic and contrapuntal ingenuities keeping the texture varied, usually with a basso ostinato supporting the whole. The polyphony is vocally derived.

Bruckner does not seek God; he has found Him. He is content to praise God; then, his devotions over, he enjoys the *Heimat* of his scherzo, which he does heartily, not like Mahler, looking back nostalgically to a lost innocence and world of *Wunderhorn*. The classic roots of Bruckner are not German; his polyphony stems from Palestrina rather than from Bach. He was not in the German symphonic line; he was not, though an Austrian and a dweller in Vienna, a follower of Schubert. Despite certain first-movement technical and expository traits in his first movements which recall Beethoven, and despite a D minor adagio method similar to that of the slow movement of the 'Choral' Symphony, Bruckner is not Beethovenish in his view of music, or in his psychological make-up. He has neither Beethoven's range of imagination nor his tremendous smithy. There is no anvil in Bruckner, no hammer, no white-heat. Bruckner's music is sturdy, without protest or rebelliousness. It is sure of itself even if it stumbles, which frequently it does. Every symphony of Bruckner is a mountain, moved very much by faith.

It is one of the ironies of musical history that Bruckner should have fallen among Wagnerians. They used him in the controversy with Brahms; they set him up in a high place, as they thought. They even altered his orchestration, making a Bruckner adagio sound like the 'Trauersmarsch', and his first movement climaxes like the cohorts of Wotan entering Walhall. Varied nature herself could not make two men as unlike as Wagner and Bruckner in essential stuff. Bruckner, 'half God, half simpleton', as Mahler called him, the non-erotic (musically) Bruckner, never protean and always Anton – what has he the slightest in common with the composer of *Tristan*, *Parsifal*, the creator of Kundry, Brünnhilde, Siegfried, Hagen, Hans Sachs? Bruckner was drawn fervently to Wagner's music, nevertheless Wagner was his anti-Christ, if only he had known it!

II

The instrumental symphony came to consummation with Haydn and Mozart. Beethoven fertilized it with drama and humanity; and the denouement was achieved by power of heroic conception of man's destiny. Beethoven created what the Germans called the *Apotheosis Finale*. But from Beethoven the classical symphony branched away in two broad directions: Mendelssohn, Schumann and Brahms gave it the stamp and flavour of the *Mittel-Deutsch* bourgeoisie. After his first symphony, Brahms avoided the 'Apotheosis' finale and the heroic gesture; the finale of his fourth and last symphony is strictly a musical apotheosis. Mendelssohn, Schumann and Brahms each composed German music of the middle classes; and they observed the symphonic logic of the great school in which they were nurtured. Schumann's adventurings with a connecting theme and a continuous procedure of tone from one movement to the next was in no way a flirtation with the symphonic-poem's illustrative purposes. Bruckner did not grow from this branch. With Schubert was born the Austrian symphony, not heroic or ethical but inspired by nature worship, with romantic implications. To the Schubert symphony Bruckner brought not a 'Menschlichkeit' feeling, not a call to the awakening if not embracing millions. He brought a religious note deeply felt, patient and trustful; and though it was a personal note, he expressed it without a hint of the egoistic attitude and romanticism. He was not a romantic; his Catholicism has no *Dies Irae*, no winding-sheets and no charnel houses. It is generally a gemütlich spiritual experience we are given by Bruckner, exalting us but never inflaming our minds with awful visions. Outside his own country, Bruckner has had a chequered posterity. No Italian could sit through music as untheatrical as a Bruckner symphony or a Bruckner Mass. No Frenchman could listen for long to music so little connected with the world of wit and women as Bruckner's. German-Austrian conductors have introduced Bruckner to America. In England he is gradually proving that he is not merely long-winded and platitudinous, though, as a fact, he is not infrequently both. The stumbling-block is, of course, the long extent of Bruckner's movements, portentous and discursive, the whole passing slowly and monumentally. Even in an opening allegro Bruckner is unhurried, static.

Of course, the duration of a Bruckner symphony is connected with the character and extent of the material treated, and to the way the mind of the composer works. It was an original mind. The simplicity of Bruckner has been overdone; it was a simplicity of nature, not of musical imagination. The argument and syntax, the unfolding and folding of a Bruckner symphony asks for close and intent musical thinking; his logic is less formal than that of say Brahms. It is even a relaxation to attend to Brahms's compartmental exposition, development and recapitulation technique after following Bruckner along his labyrinthine ways. We are not able confidently to go through a Bruckner movement guided by the recognizable first-subject and second-subject finger-posts, each unmistakably marking the crossroads. A Bruckner 'subject' is usually a group of themes, two or three themes, the sequence of the group making it hard to separate one theme from another. Roughly, Bruckner's ground-plan of a first movement is this: Statement, A B C; development; A B C, A modulating into the recapitulation, as a climax not as a mechanical recall. Bruckner's enlargement of symphonic-form, his two- or three-theme groupings in expositions, which naturally demand space for development; his structure by a key-sequence very much his own; his comprehensive patient view; his sudden changes from loud to soft; his contrasts of full organ tone and solitary wood-wind echoes; his use of silence as a reinforcement of expression – all these are traits of the style that is the man. We should try to understand them and to realize that a redundance here and there, an obvious device such as an inversion, dragged in to keep things going in a sticky moment, are inevitable characteristics endearing in time, like a greying hair, a stoop, a limp, even a stammer. These things don't go deep – and Bruckner has deeps worth our while to plumb.

Not only is Bruckner at once known by his way of stating and developing his case; his tone is immediately recognizable, even a common chord or interval of a fifth. The tone is, as we have seen, sometimes very like an organ tone. The instruments are interchanged in the manner of the organist's registration. We can almost see Bruckner pulling out the stops. To ears fresh to Bruckner, the abrupt silences may well imply that the structure is insecure, that Bruckner has lost the thread of his discourse. A silence in Bruckner is called in German an *Atempause*; a pause to take in breath. Bruckner himself said that when he wanted to say something especially significant it was necessary for him first of all to create a silence. An intake of breath! – inspiration literally. While Bruckner thus meditates and is still, we might bear in mind, if we are of the heathens, George Henry Lewes's story of the drying-up of Goethe in a speech; but Goethe was not embarrassed. He simply turned his mind's eye within himself and waited five minutes until his next idea occurred to him. The intensity of his meditation held his audience spellbound. So must it seem in the great silences in a Bruckner symphony. The conductor must see to it that during the tone-pause the rhythmic pulse can unmistakably be heard. In the chapel of St Florian, resonance sustained the tone when Bruckner cut off a great swell. When he composed for orchestra he still heard music in his sudden silences.

III

The Bruckner symphonies move along much the same track. Usually the beginning is a string tremolo, a sort of pedal. Then we hear a call, probably a brass descent of a fifth, a quintuple rhythm; Dr Redlich has called this call a 'signal'. Let us be picturesque and respond to it as a 'Fiat lux'. Out of the subterranean embryo the music emerges and germ-notes assume the groups, the whole propelled by ascending and descending scales, Jacob's ladders. The main episode ends in a full close. Then comes the counter group, and the contrast is occasionally disillusioning for a while. Wood-wind echoes of cadences already heard, while plucked strings mark time, suggest a fall of temperature. Sir Thomas Beecham described his reactions to a Bruckner movement in pungent language: 'I counted six pregnancies and five miscarriages.' It needs an optimistic analysis of a Bruckner first movement to set out to persuade us that Bruckner's grip never faltered, even if the analysis should be as academically exact as one by Dr Redlich: 'The first movement [of the Ninth Symphony] represents even thematically the sum-total of Bruckner's D minor world of tragic expression. In subtlety of harmonization, exploitation of the relationship of the mediants, and also in the adventurous use of wide interval-skips ... all three completed movements surpass anything previously written by Bruckner. Harmonic teasers such as the famous initial chord of the scherzo, the Neapolitan dissonance in the concluding bar of Movement I, and the ecstatic shout by the horns in the ambit of a ninth, in the adagio ...' The point is the distinction, or lack of it, in the material handled. Bruckner's material frankly is frequently far from distinguished. Unisons, running scale-wise, detached cadences given fresh registration, persistent repetitions of fanfares – there is much of these reach-me-downs. A great long-spanned tune, self contained, is not common in Bruckner. A melody as immediately convincing, a heavenly visitation, such as the cantabile 3/4 string theme of the adagio of the Seventh Symphony, is scarce in Bruckner. Like all composers not capable of inventing long-spanned melodies, Bruckner is reduced to the last and great resort of polyphony and all the devices of inversions, augmentation and so forth. The thing hard to explain is that most times he asserts himself; genius makes good a shortage of talent.

It is easy while discussing Bruckner to fall into contradiction or apparent inconsistency. If we are walking on a mountainside we are likely to come across at least a few barren stretches leading nowhere, then the broad view unfolds the wonderful vista. It happens like this as we traverse the range of Bruckner symphonies. I have just expressed the opinion that Bruckner was not a fruitful melodist; and the Fifth Symphony will support me here. But the adagio of the Eighth Symphony looms again before me, the most rapt, heartfelt, slow movement since the adagio of Beethoven's Ninth. But is this great movement compact really of melody, or is it not by a consummate art of cadence and echo, of beautiful harmonic contrast and interchange of the organ stops, that Bruckner erects a 'Heilige Halle' of tones calling to tones from the depths to the heights? The beginning of the movement has been likened to that of 'O sink hernieder' in the love duet of the second act of *Tristan und Isolde*; and there is momentarily the same hush, the same throb in the gently syncopated string harmonies. But if the passage is any relation at all to Tristan and Isolde it is one without sex. This music, plummet-sounding, is 'beyond these voices'; the throb turns to a spreading glow as the full orchestra becomes radiant, the sun on the mountain at dawn. We need the German language to describe the metamorphosis; 'das ganze Orchester in strahlenden A-dur in hohe Regionen emporschwebt' (the quotation is from Werner Wolff's admirable study: *Anton Bruckner – Genie und Einfalt*). The main theme of this movement consists of two elements or germ-cells, and in the first statement of it opulent sweeps of the harp suspend the cadence. The reiterations are not mechanical now. If ever Orsino should have cried 'That strain again', it is in the course of this Adagio. But it isn't the food of earthly love; rather it is the love of the gods as they remember some existence on the lowly, friendly and passionate earth. Another contradiction which trips the commentator on Bruckner is the existence in his music, almost side by side, of the prosaic and the poetic. Prose – I mean good and noble prose cast in long paragraphs – gives way to sensitive coloured measures of rich strings and horns evocative of distant fields – Elysian probably. Maybe these moments in Bruckner when he forgets his godhead and becomes an ordinary mortal genius are less metrical poetry than blank verse of potent imaginative voltage, as in the slow movement of the Eighth Symphony. The elaboration of this movement, its paragraphs and parentheses, its simple plastic generating motion, its absolute originality of thought and method, constitute one of the abiding beauties of nineteenth-century music.

The outer movements of the Eighth Symphony and the Scherzo are fine enough, but the Adagio inevitably stands as a lonely peak; self-contained perhaps, rather than lonely. The first movement, though, is an astonishing example of Bruckner's power to build mightily out of sequences, imitations, repeated short insistent note-groups, contrasts of weight and spareness, culminating as usual in a blazing fanfare reinforced by striding brass. The Scherzo, too, is a tour de force of rhythmical persistence; but the long mazeful trio is entirely unlike any other contrasting middle section ever given to a scherzo. The more we study Bruckner the more we should guard against confusing the man's simplicity of heart and intelligence with the musical instincts which led him into involutions of thought, always symphonic, compared with which the thinking of a Brahms, an Elgar, a Vaughan Williams, is direct and immediately made logically clear to the plainest mind. There was in Bruckner that subtlety of introspection and independence of explanatory verbal clauses that is often the mark of solitary and not sophisticated men.

From the Fifth to the Ninth Symphonies, Bruckner concentrated on the adagio as the structural and emotional culmination, leaving himself with little to do in the finale, except make music. He seeks to link his finale to the whole by thematic connection, but after the tension of the adagio a sense of anticlimax sets in. It is a matter of opinion which of the Bruckner symphonies has the greatest or greater adagio; each is unparalleled since Beethoven for profound and varied introspection. As I say, I chose the adagio of the Eighth Symphony, but there is the poignant 'Vale' of the Ninth, the piercing beauty of the cry of the heart of the Sixth, with its pathetic oboes, the processional grandeur of the Seventh. Bruckner was an adagio man; his quick movements, we have seen, tend to suggest a congenital slowness of gait, physical and mental, temporarily speeded-up. The ruminations of Bruckner in these adagios inspires key-relationships unprecedented at the time of their composition. Never do they interpose between us and the raptness of the expression. They are not exploited demon-stratively; they lift veil after veil on the deepening note of trust and the mystery of the spiritual. In a Bruckner adagio, clause is succeeded by sub-clause; the music turns inward. The argument is not easy to follow. Like religion and matrimony, Bruckner needs faith.

IV

Again we must not be too sure in our generalizations about Bruckner. He was a lonely man, as far as a man can be lonely having Bruckner's love of God; he lived a lonely life. As a composer he had no school, no ancestry and no successors. But though he pursued a single track, it was a mountain on which he meandered; consequently his view could be extensive enough. He is a very humane composer; his Catholicism does not breed a separating mysticism. He worships without ritual, incense or any hint of sacerdotal-ism. He has humours which because wit does not sharpen any edge keep him perpetually likeable. No composer invites a more friendly response than Bruckner; even his recurrent prolixity is engaging, for the simple reason that he doesn't seem to care whether we are listening to him or not. His scherzi are 'frisks' and fatherly. Dr Johnson would enjoy them. He tries to dance with us. The tumult of his outer movements, the stride of brass and the grandeur of an orchestral great-swell, create the impression of pageantry, not a pageantry of pomp and circumstance (Bruckner's love of country never ran to Elgar's patriotism), but of gusto for the visible sensible world, mantle of invisible God. If his music is never erotic, it is not without a love of all creatures, love of Adam as well as of Eve, but in an Eden that has grown no sophisticated apple. If ever a composer was a good man it was Bruckner; the naivety of this expression suits the case.

We can also overdo the organist influence in Bruckner's technique. His orchestration is masterful, with a sure ear for instrumental character. His judgment of dynamics is seldom at fault. He opens the heart of wood-wind; his brass is majestic or stirringly triumphant in turn, never merely brilliant or spectacular. His writing for strings, especially lower strings, is beautifully nuanced and harmonized. The Bruckner tone is weighty on the whole; the suggestions of organ registration do not lead to any impurity or weakening of the Bruckner orchestral tissue, which is absolutely masculine. We can overdo, too, the controversy about original and revised editions of Bruckner. The core and essence of what Bruckner had to say to us is not crucially affected by the presence or absence of cymbal clashes or choirs of tubas. Even Bruckner's own revisions throughout his lifetime did not change fundamental stuff. A blasting operating on a mountainside leaves the face of the land more or less unchanged after a year or two. His material contains nothing with a banal association. The simplest ingredient is untouched by the dross of the world. He remained apart from the romantic movement of his period and all its indulgences, histrionic or real. He opened no fresh paths, or was not aware of them if he himself did happen to wander along new paths. Here, maybe, lies his greatness, which no neglect can hurt. A mountain is none the worse if only a few, with aid of the right stamina and persistence, have climbed it.

v
Gustav Mahler
1860-1911

Gustav Mahler

GUSTAV MAHLER was an Austrian and a Jew who became converted to Catholicism. He composed ten symphonies of large dimension, and also he was one of the great conductors of music's history. He wrote not a note that recalls the harsh patriarchal accents of Hebraism; there is no incense in his work; on the contrary, he worships nature and mankind as much as he worships the Church of the Blessed Virgin.

He was born tragically. The gods lavished gifts on him which blossomed in many directions. They gave him imagination and intellect; they gave him the passion of devotion and emulation; also they gave him the Jew's restless self-consciousness and egoism. The priest and the artist in him were made kin with the actor, for conducting, after all, is a form of acting. His boyhood was shadowed by cruelty. His father and mother hated each other and jealously fed on his love; two brothers and a sister were doomed to suicide, madness or deceit. He lived for a while on his mother and she on him; then his daemon awoke and he was driven into the greater world to independence ruthless and savage. At the age of thirty-eight he was dictator of music of Central Europe in the Imperial Opera of Vienna at the full noon of its splendour. His pursuit of truth and beauty was fanatical, and in the end the world broke him. With a character and temperament woven from rare and sensitive strands into a bodeful twisted texture, he was at variance with himself from the beginning. Today he stands as a typical figure of romanticism; he was also the first of the examples of pathological musical genius; and he was the symbol of the frustration of the Jew in music. He was a great man, both in himself and because of the way he was used by the Time Spirit. He deserves patient study, aesthetic and psychological.

II

We run into entanglements of his mind and art at the first glance of a score of Mahler. The material of the music is often familiar and simple; the organization of it, the technique of form and transition, is original and complex. Melodies from the Bohemian countryside are recollected against a background of medieval demon-lore; the child in Mahler is always running to his mother's apron to hide. In the Fourth Symphony, where paradise is seen as a place of gilt and gingerbreads, a vision passes of Death sitting with his tuneless fiddle on a gravestone. Cuckoo-calls, bugle-calls from barracks at dawn; the march of the gay noisy bands of Vienna; an ancient chorale or an echo from his beloved masters, Beethoven, Bruckner, Schubert – all these remembered strains and cadences are changed to sophisticated inflexions and texture. Folk-song in wood-wind is answered by the romantic rhetoric of horn and brass. Into a tone-world of Styrian landscape and old village comes the languishing and over-civilized string portamento of the city and concert house, dripping with Zärtlichkeit. The trombones perform audacities of chromatic scales; and the timpani is an arsenal. Naive, you say, without pausing to consider whether a Jew can ever be naive. But look further into this music; take the whole of a Mahler symphony in a survey from beginning to end. Elaboration and extension could not easily go beyond Mahler's. He freed symphonic logic and syntax from many traditional inhibitions; he extended the movements, and made fantasias of development-sections. He bred thematic material like pond-life; he transformed symphonic melody into the arabesque of improvisation. He clarified the symphonic harmony, for Mahler's orchestra was not made numerous for sonority's sake; he needed many instruments because he aimed at and achieved characteristic colour, the intimate line. There is no harmony, he said, only counterpoint. He, in fact, was orchestrally the link between romantic orchestral harmony and the linear instrumentation of the present day. In the technique of symphonic organization Brahms was the naive composer, compared with Mahler. Yet at bottom, in his thematic stuff, and also in the conceptions underlying his music, Mahler remained for long the Mahler who wrote the 'Lieder eines fahrenden Gesellen', the composer who heard the wonder-horn of youth in his ears, until the great seas of his age's romanticism lured him from the land.

He once described himself as Strauss's antithesis. There is some truth in it; Strauss had all the invention and Mahler had all the aspiration. In the decline and fall and renewal of Strauss there was irony; in the noble reach that exceeded the grasp of Mahler there was pathos. Strauss was of this world, and Mahler, as he sang in his own song, was lost in the world: 'Ich bin der Welt abhanden gekommen.' Throughout his music, even in the Christmas-card view of a peasant's heaven depicted in the Fourth Symphony, a refrain from this song can be heard. It was the Mahler leit-motif, his essential cadence; and it came to a dying fall and end in 'Das Lied von der Erde'.

He was at one and the same time egoist and Everyman. He wrote the first autobiographical symphonies; but he wrote, too, the Eighth Symphony, dedicated to humanity. There he saw as in a vision a universal music which would

praise heaven and earth with a thousand voices and instruments, the fields and the birds of the air, the smallest of
earth's creatures, and men and women and children. Not
the stern ethical millennium of Beethoven did Mahler wish
to proclaim, but the world of here and now, made sweeter
with love of brother and brother, of sister and sister, of
father and son, of mother and child. There is no love
expressed in Mahler except love of kind. In his ten symphonies we can follow the journey of the man's soul and its
struggles. The first four of them show us the emergence
from youth to maturity; the echoes of Mahler's home and
countryside can still be heard as he plunges into the greater
world and lives through the Sturm und Drang which in
those days was the aesthetic fashion shaping the artist's life.
The Mahler symphonies are a close sequence, and not until
the Tenth can we see how the wheel of the man comes full
circle. In the Fifth, Sixth and Seventh Symphonies Mahler
composed without using words or the human voice, his only
wordless and unvocal music since the First Symphony. He
was now at the height of his career as musician and master
of the orchestra, and the Fifth, Sixth and Seventh of his
symphonies are the first full fruits of his orchestral culture.

The Eighth Symphony, the 'Symphony of a Thousand',
reveals Mahler placing his art, now that he is technically a
master, at the service of all people. 'Mir heisst Symphonie',
was his credo, 'mit allen Mitteln der vorhandenen Technik,
mir eine Welt aufbauen.' He would bequeath his inheri-
tance to the world. The Eighth Symphony embraces, in
intention at any rate, earth and heaven; the music speaks
not of the individual but of the universal soul. The
enormous choir and orchestra are as the time-and-space
dimension; and fresh young voices relate birth to experience
as they lisp and choir, as young angels, of the blessed
children born into the loftier ether. Eight soloists share the

burden, like so many Atlases, of supporting Mahler's universe of song and tone.

Then, after the Eighth Symphony, a complete reaction, an escape from the rejoicing multitude, to loneliness. Mahler could not himself enter the world of Everyman. In the Eighth Symphony the apotheosis proclaims, to the words of Goethe, the fulfilment of all things. Here is realized the unrealizable:

> Das Unbeschreibliche,
> Hier ist es getan.

But not for Mahler the brotherhood of heaven on earth. He was not of the masses; and he was still at war with himself as man and artist. He turns away in his next work, his masterpiece, from all that he has been heading for, from the vision he saw of a music which would be now a dream, now a drama, now a song of nature, now a song of man, now a dance and now a sermon. He was always a wanderer in the world. Not as a master of magnitude in music could he find his soul; he could not return again to mere music. Not again as the revealing priest in a truly Catholic cathedral of tone could he speak. These experiences an artist can go through but once, and if he then finds not what he seeks he must look elsewhere. Mahler saved himself and achieved his masterpiece, not in the symphony of his own ego; not in the symphony of Everyman; not even in the symphony of remembered youth; and not in the réclame of opera and concert. He wrote freely and happily and beautifully out of a soul at peace at last, out of an imagination at one with itself and fully realized, when he went into the hills and absorbed a philosophy and poetry of ancient China, expressing acquiescence, fortified by wine and fancy, and nature's loneliness that gently falls over the ego like a cloak.

I cannot think of Mahler as a man who just sat down and composed symphonies and offered them for our delectation simply as music. With each of his works he lived through a necessary stage in his spiritual development. Music was his only way of life. He had to shed many skins. He needed to create music to fulfil his destiny, as a woman needs children, at the risk of producing masterpieces or not masterpieces.

'So closely bound up is the act of creation in me with all my experience that when my mind and spirit are at rest I can compose nothing.' Also he said: 'When I conceive a composition I always arrive at the point where I must employ the word as the bearer of my musical idea.' It is important, at once, to realize exactly what the 'word' meant for Mahler; it is the crudest error to infer that he ever wrote programme-music; this fact had best be understood before our studies in Mahler proceed farther. The use of the human voice and words in Mahler no more sunders him from the symphonic style than the use of words sunders Beethoven from it in the Ninth. There are, as I say, refrains and cadences in the Mahler symphonies of songs he heard or composed in youth or in early manhood; they follow him even into the harder and more bony world of his instrumental symphonies, the Fifth, Sixth and Seventh. But as soon as a melody of vocal origin enters Mahler's mind it is, if I may use the word, symphonized: it loses its independence as song and becomes a theme, a motif, a germ of an instrumental texture. Sometimes, he seems not to have taken the trouble to invent his symphonic material. And we arrive now at the celebrated problem of his banality, his Banalität.

III

Romain Rolland has written cynically of Mahler's 'assimilations', of 'Beethoven taking lessons from Mendelssohn; Chabrier giving Bach a helping hand'. This is superficial, a classic example of 'Banalität' in musical criticism. For Mahler is one of the most personal of composers; his music, even when it recalls other music, is stamped unmistakably with his own style, his own way of feeling. His shallowest detractors contradict themselves; they dismiss him as a conductor who composed from memory helped out by a conductor's technique of instrumentation, and then they admit that they are repelled by the Mahler *Stimmung*, the Mahler temperament. I cannot only *feel* Mahler in nearly every bar he wrote; I can see him. His music seems to project the essence of him, a sort of ectoplasm. I am not concerned here with likes or dislikes; I am pointing out that whether you love or detest Mahler, he exists. The trouble is that much has been written or said of Mahler by people who do not know his music; they have heard only the so-called banalities, those parts of his speech belonging to the common musical vocabulary of his period. I can imagine that Bach in *his* day was accused of banality; I mean that his melody and harmony were much in the air; he made an inherited stock of material his own by drawing it through the sieve of his mind.

Mahler lived all his days in music; for music he burnt himself out at an early age. Of the great composers – and make no mistake, he is great – he is the only one who conceived, thought and experienced mainly in symphonic terms. He wrote no opera, though he was the greatest of all conductors of opera; and he wrote no piano or chamber music; even his song cycles are symphonically felt, at bottom. Into one form of music he poured his consciousness as man and artist; through one form of music he sought to untie the knot intrinsicate of his being. Not since Beethoven had a composer aimed at a larger and more truly symphonic ideal than Mahler's. And the essence of the symphony is the transition, the experience, the denouement – not the birth and starting-point. I suspect that for Mahler the very elements of music, the language of it, often possessed a significance in themselves, enriched by association; he perhaps felt that melodic invention was not his strong point. Often after he has got a new idea he is compelled to foster it and nourish it with all his instrumental sophistication and dexterity. In the Eighth Symphony, when he is hymning the song of all the children of God and nature, he is no more concerned with originality of theme than the priest devotedly performing a traditional ritual; the old hallowed modes and inflexions serve well enough. Through music he had to go his ways; all that he found on the journey, all that he inherited, he made his own by thought and intense feeling. In Mahler the style is not the idiom, the harmony, the structure; it is the man himself.

He composed, as I say, the first autobiographical symphonies. In Beethoven the hero is humanity seen in heroic mould; the Beethoven symphony is ethical and presents the struggle of idealism with destiny. There is no egoism in Beethoven. The Liszt and Berlioz symphonic-poem presented a romantic type – Byronic, presented objectively as Harold or Mazeppa or Faust. Brahms emulated the Beethoven ethic in his First Symphony, then contented himself with music of reflective fancy or subjective feeling. The D major, F major and E minor Symphonies of Brahms are not really more symphonic than any of the first of Haydn's London set; I mean that they speak no ethic, no credo, certainly tell of no *Weltanschauung*. They are technically symphonies, of course; they are, as a fact, a superb adaptation of the old suite to a richer musical equipment. When we consider the symphonies of Brahms or of Sibelius, for example, we do not feel that after the composition of any of them, the composition of another marked an inevitable direction, even a crisis, in the life of either of these composers, as men, not only as artists. If the Third Symphony of Brahms had followed the First, none of us would have felt a sense of a gap or hiatus anywhere in Brahms's spiritual development. But Mahler could not possibly have conceived, let alone have written, 'Das Lied von der Erde' earlier than he did write it; he had to seek it hard and patiently. Each of his symphonies was for Mahler a shedding of a skin; a renewal or renunciation. The finale of one symphony of Mahler presupposes the beginning of its successor. When the whole set of them was performed at Amsterdam some forty years ago, we could understand that here, if there was much that could not be regarded as great music, there was not an insignificant note. It was as though a noble and defeated man were being self-portrayed before us; it was an incarnation of Mahler; the mental suffering stuff of him, the bones and perishable flesh had long since been flung into the earth. In these vast corridors of music his ghost walked still seeking, hearing now echoes of poignant beauty, now of long lost happiness, now of brave striding forging music, now of the whole heavens choiring to the bright-eyed cherubim; then suddenly sounded the chord of frustration of the earthbound, the dissonance that was all Mahler's experience crystallized into tone, even the banalities which made him, or should have made him, Everyman's composer.

IV

We do not land ourselves into contradiction if we agree that Mahler was sincere and yet an actor, and that his music is thoroughly symphonic yet full of dramatic or self-conscious gestures. It is the nature of the symphony to unfold a drama. The greatest of the Beethoven symphonies, the 'Eroica', the Fifth and the Ninth, tell of a problem that from a preliminary antinomy, challenge and clash of motives, achieves a solution. The movements mount to a clinching peak; there is a crescendo, not a decrescendo of the symphonic tone and dynamic. Mahler in none of his symphonies leaves us or himself at the point where he began; he does not, as Brahms does in the Second, Third and Fourth Symphonies, give us only an accumulation of rich musical material. He differs from Beethoven by his personal participation in the drama; he is not in the Beethoven succession really. His lineage is with the C major Symphony of Schubert, in which a romantic connection is felt between man and nature.

He was the born actor in his finales, which are usually 'effective', the whole orchestra taking the curtain or fade-out. No; there is nothing insincere about the Mahler apotheosis; the gesture may be aware of its purpose, none the less it is honest. As an original creative artist he had an inferiority complex; consequently he took care to arrange an imposing grouping at the right moment. Even the farewell of 'Das Lied von der Erde' is not unself-conscious; the daring repetitions at the word 'Ewig', softer and softer, with the celesta tinkling its pretty bitter-sweet, reveals that in Mahler resided the disinterested spectator of Diderot's 'Paradox of the Actor'. And here we come – as every discussion of Mahler is bound sooner or later to come – to the question of his naivety. The conceptions behind much of Mahler's work at first strike us as childlike or childish. There is the Fourth Symphony's gilt and gingerbread picture of a paradise where the Austrian peasants see eternity not in a blade of grass but in a vegetable garden with haloed gardeners. The angels bake the bread while

Sankt Peter in Himmel sicht zu.

This symphony is woven from the most homely tunes by the subtle and nicely calculated instrumentation of a great artificer of music. We must indeed know what we intend the word 'naive' to mean before we apply it to Mahler. If we turn from our consideration of him for a moment and take a glance at Bruckner, the most naive of composers, we are bound to confess that if Mahler also can be called naive the term is capable of generous accommodation. Bruckner was undoubtedly naive; he was simple of heart and simple of technique. There was nothing clever about him; he was unsophisticated and would not have dared to use the Mahler portamento or appoggiatura. If Bruckner sometimes lost his way in a development-section, the reason was not only that he was contemplating God but that his skill was not equal to everything. Naivety implies a certain innocence, an open-eyed wonder. Mahler, with the Jew's sharp mind, never forgot himself; it was his restlessness of intellect and his gestures that prevented him from composing an adagio. Adagio, by the way, is not just a tempo indication; it denotes a mode of musical feeling. Beethoven in the Ninth Symphony fixed the adagio style once and for all. It is a sermon in music, with many turnings upon itself, many labyrinthine ways, many Firstlys, Secondlys, Thirdlys; in fact, many Tenthlys and Lastlys. Apart from Bruckner nobody since Beethoven, except Elgar in his A flat Symphony, has composed in the adagio style. Brahms seldom got beyond a secondly, and he was lyrical not contemplative.

The adagio of the Ninth Symphony of Mahler, though it pays tribute to Bruckner, is too nervous, too sentimental in nuance, to suit the simple sublimity of the adagio style. A genuine naivety is not conscious that it is open to parody. In one or two places in his symphonies Mahler takes pains to instruct his interpreters to avoid suggestions of parody. Bruckner is never aware of exposure at any moment to parody; he does not watch his step, so to say. The artist and the actor in Mahler surveyed the nature of their material; the naive conception was artfully shaped; for example, study the 'Resurrection' episode in the Second of the Mahler symphonies. The heaven of the orchestra trumpets the bodeful summons; a flute flutters in the silence, like a nightingale in an apocalyptic dawn. The timpani booms as though out of the earth; the dead rise and march to a banal tune; but the skill of a symphonist growing to mastery connives all the material to an end which is one of the most remarkable and original in music. Mahler was a Bruckner advocate (but at the extreme in temperament and technique) and he rendered tribute to his master in his own work. But Bruckner was as the saint sent to dwell on earth for a brief space; he had not to seek and struggle to find *his* heaven as Mahler so sorely had to seek and struggle, being not naive, but complex and lost in the world.

V

Mahler was once asked to state his religious and philosophical beliefs or credo, and he replied: 'Ich bin Musiker'. He also stated that in music, whether he was creating or conducting, all questions about the meaning of the world became clear to him; indeed no questions remained to be asked. Music was all experience for Mahler. A technical explanation will not get over the fact that not until towards

116

the end of his life did his music achieve warmth of harmony. Even at the height of his mastery as a craftsman he still wrote with a bareness of melody that made the softness of a close harmony impossible. In the first movement of the Fifth Symphony there is a return to the Faustian stress and ambition of the first movement of the Second Symphony; the expression is actually bonier; and in the great rondo fugue, which is the finale, Mahler's melody is so much contending against itself that it will not blend submissively within the give-and-take limits of polyphony. He was certainly craftsman enough when he composed the Fifth Symphony to soften, had he deliberately chosen, the jarring independence of melodic parts into a warmer harmony. But Mahler was never the man to regard music as an art to be contrived as though from the outside; if he could not feel a harmony of spirit he could not equivocate and write a dishonest musical harmony. The failure of much of his work was caused by his inability to subdue the man in him to the artist. Wordsworth was probably right to 'recollect in tranquillity' before beginning to make poetry. The rondo fugue of the Fifth Symphony is almost wilful in its complexity; Mahler, in fact, was compelled to readjust the instrumental parts; he went beyond his own command of orchestral ensemble. (Yet in the same work he could give us the saccharine adagietto.) In much of the writing of Mahler's middle-period, from the Fifth to the Seventh Symphonies, there is a suspicion of a challenge to Strauss in the shape of multitudinous and vaunting melody; but Mahler was the more serious composer of the two – he could not wear an orchestral coat of many colours for its own sake.

The first skin, the skin of youth and early manhood, was shed after the composition of the Fourth Symphony. From now onward Mahler glances back only as a mature philosophic man linking past to present with a sense of the pathos of distance, or for the purposes of ironic contrast. The music ceases to sing of nature as a present or a remembered joy; the 'Wunderhorn' songs and childhood are outgrown. When they are echoed or simulated, as in the Seventh Symphony, where the 'Revelge' march grimly stalks through the 'Nachtmusik', the intent is to dramatize or poetize later and deeper experiences. The main vocally-born motif in Mahler's symphonic melody henceforth is derived from the Rückert song, 'Ich bin der Welt abhanden gekommen', far removed from the wonder-horn of youth. With the Fourth Symphony behind him Mahler's technique becomes more and more contrapuntal, or rather he depends less and less on any dominant theme, but gives his instrumental parts separate identity, so that freedom and indeqendence of line and movement produce a harder texture, where harmony is not flesh but bone, with no luxurious indulgence in chords for romantic purposes. Pedal-points and bare fourths and fifths make the Mahler flavours aseptic. Mahler is now no longer nostalgic but in fact forward-looking in a way that can be called ethical and visionary. The first exploratory movements of the Fifth, Sixth and Seventh Symphonies seem to urge and press to a sought goal, and the middle sections can be described as symphonic battle-fields. The use of march and Ländler rhythms in these instrumental symphonies must not mislead us into thinking that Mahler is yet again escaping to the past and its memories; march and Ländler rhythms point to instrumental as much as to vocal origins.

There is material for long fascinating study in these symphonies of transition; for the Fifth, Sixth and Seventh are bridges from one Mahler to a greater Mahler. He is trying to integrate his imagination and experience, trying to make a synthesis of the poet, the visionary, the idealist and the man of musical action who in the opera house always knew what he wanted and got it. If we bear in mind that Mahler's symphonies, ten of them of immense range and reach, were composed in the spare time of the career of a conductor as great and extensive as Toscanini himself, and that he died before his fifty-first birthday, we shall perhaps be able to realize the psychological significance of a certain stylistic dichotomy in Mahler, who, as he once said, never wrote an insincere note. The histrionic gesture even recurs in the Eighth Symphony at the spiritual height of the second and Goethe movement. The appearance of the Mater Gloriosa is set to a rather cloyingly sweet swaying melody for soft violins, with arpeggios for harp and harmonium, angelical enough for Gounod; it is an operatic apotheosis, yet it is so imaginatively related to the context, and the context is so superbly conceived as a whole, that our taste does not condemn the response of our easily allured ears. When Mahler went to New York, after Vienna had shamefully jockeyed him out of the State Opera, he for the first time in his life found himself in charge of a symphony orchestra, free of duties in the theatre. He confessed that if earlier in his career as a composer he had been able to sink his mind entirely in symphonic music the scores of his own masterpieces might have contained fewer impurities. The closing section of the Eighth Symphony is cleared of scenic or limelit associations by the exalted 'Blicket auf', and the wonderful setting of 'Alles Vergängliches'. If Mahler had composed no other music than this we should have guessed of his genius.

In one of the most illuminating sentences about Mahler ever written, Dr Redlich[1] has argued that 'this cosmic aspect of the Symphony led Mahler to conceive motifs, so to speak, more than life-size and of long-range power. They

---

[1] H. F. Redlich, *Bruckner and Mahler* (J. M. Dent).

were intended to be used as projectiles capable of piercing the hearts of the most distant listeners and of being effectively reproduced by a multitude of sound media'. But Mahler never wrote merely for effect. The dimensions of his orchestra, and the duration of certain of his movements, are not evidence of a Teuton worship of size and verbose rhetoric. His long movements are the logical consequence of the symphonic content, the material under treatment. The subjects or themes are not spatially compact; a single statement in an exposition is a group of themes, not a sentence or paragraph but a whole 'period'; consequently the development is proportionately elaborate, with extended and never repetitive recapitulation. It is the grossest error to accuse Mahler of structural insecurity or diffusive thinking. The logic of Mahler's thinking is fierce in its rightness; his handling of complex form is firm, even if it has the vehemence of a man wrestling with beasts. But we must avoid overdoing the daemonic side of Mahler's genius; he wrote plenty of music of charm and allurement and of light fanciful touch. The 'Andante Amoroso' of the Seventh Symphony is so enchanting in its rich scoring, a confection of strings, wood-wind, horn, mandolin and guitar, that I am at a loss why it isn't one of the most popular symphonic movements in the whole range of music.

VI

In 'Das Lied von der Erde' we come to one of the great transitions in the history of any artist's spiritual journey; and of course the style is changed proportionately. Maybe in the first song or movement of the work ('Trinklied vom Jammer der Erde'), some old distress and disunity remain; the key is Mahler's favourite tragic key – A minor. There is a reckless defiance in the flourish of four horns at the beginning; there is mocking and stinging pizzicato; there is a nervous tremolo; the solo voice grapples against the orchestra's rhetorical drunken dynamics. Then we enter the twilight of the second movement ('Der Einsame im Herbst'). The tone is suddenly reduced to the scale of orchestral miniature; beauty passes like shadows over the cool lake of Mahler's tone. Life, the music says now, is but a reflection, and will not last. The third movement ('Von der Jugend') is the scherzo. The composer enchants us to a pathetically lovely and fragile cloud-cuckoo land; delicate china porcelain is transmuted to tone, 'like the tiger's back arches the bridge of jade, and in the pavilion friends are sitting, beautifully dressed ... some are writing verses. The half-moon is in the water, upside down; all is reflected in the water'. Mahler catches the image in his orchestra; such a magic of dancing melody as this has seldom visited music; the alchemy of it all is done by the power of genius. There is a remarkable visual sense employed in the fourth movement ('Von der Schönheit'), a companion-piece to the Chinese Pavilion. Young maidens pluck flowers, and horses charge and rear decoratively; the orchestral art by which Mahler creates his illusion is here absolutely certain, and employed with the most precise judgment of each instrument's own colour and of its suitability for blending into a tinted whole. In the fifth movement, the tenor again extols the grape; but there is no tumult or challenge this time. 'Is life a dream; why labour and worry?' A bird sings on the bough; Mahler twitters his oboe and then sweetens us with his own characteristic string-crescendo, beginning, of course, 'ritard', followed by 'langsam'; the whole (naturally!) 'zurückhaltend'.

The finale, the 'Abschied', is a long slow movement, almost imperceptibly diversified – recitative, funeral march, and lyrical and passionate leavetaking, which seems to put beauty and regret into the wine-press of the orchestra and squeeze out the last juices. The vocal writing in the recitative sections awakens the secret places of loneliness. The wood-wind flutters in a world of sunset and valediction. It is music that seems to listen and wait. A voice emphasizes the stillness. At the climax, the lees of ache for lost beauty are exuded: 'Wo bleibst du? Du lässt mich lang allein?' The rising arches of the vocal part, at the words: 'O Schönheit ... O ewigen Liebens ... Lebens ... trunk'ne Welt', and the descent, with the orchestra's antiphony of strings rising and falling into an intense appoggiatura – I know no music more heart-wounding than this as an expression of longing for far-off loveliness; not even the 'Nur einmal, ach; nur einmal noch' of Isolde. Now comes the funeral march or dirge, which in my opinion makes all other funeral marches or dirges merely so many public ceremonials or State occasions for the expression of a commonplace grief, with pall-bearers and all. Out of Mahler's chasm of emptiness, the voice asks: 'Where do you go and why?' The recitative is remote: Mahler instructs that it should be sung without expression; but he himself has seen to it that no irrelevance of emotion could possibly be put into the vocal writing here. It is recitative that seems to make a ghost of the speech-accentuation to which it shapes itself. It is the recitative not of resignation but of rapt and ready submission. No bird-song flutters now from the wood-wind in the silver grey twilight of Mahler's orchestra. Not even Debussy has conjured a stillness like this of Mahler's; it is not the silence of mysterious haunts of the spirit; it is silence of a tired human heart content at last to surrender to sleep. 'Wohin ich geh'? Ich geh', ich wand're in die Berge.' To the mountain and to the Heimat. The strings and harp glimmer through the mists; and with a simple change to C major, the music sings the swan-song: 'The dear earth blossoms everywhere.' The main melody of the 'Abschied', derived from the theme of the 'Trunklied', where the singer dreams of the blue heaven and the everlasting springtime, is simplified. There is no appoggiatura in it now, no restlessness, no excess of passion. The voice withdraws to the silence: 'Ewig; Ewig.' Oboe and flute seem to hold the last faint echoes from the hills; in the deep night of the orchestra, trombones and strings intone the earth-embracing C major; and we cannot say exactly at what moment the work ends.

In conception and art, the 'Abschied' is amongst the unique things of music. The score is original; even the device of the appoggiatura is as though transformed to a fresh key for the opening of unknown casements. The instrumental technique of Mahler was perhaps the most elaborate that any one composer has commanded; in 'Das Lied' he draws it through the sieve of a suddenly clarified mind. The large orchestra approximates at times to the style of chamber music. Every instrument is exposed in an orchestration of silverpoint. A member of the Vienna Philharmonic Orchestra once said to me: 'Mahler, in "Das Lied von der Erde", makes you feel naked.' It is in this masterpiece that his scoring is prophetic; his melody is as free as arabesque; it is not chained to a fixed system of harmony. The form makes fantasias in sonata-sequence; Mahler in his maturity was one of the most imaginative and free moulders or weavers of the symphonic tissue that music has so far known. Compared with him, most of his contemporaries speak to us in the short-breathed compact syntax of minds which can employ only brief and closely juxtaposed paragraphs.

To the critics of Mahler who have declared that 'Das Lied' is a pastiche, I would quote only one example of his genius for germination and synthesis. A three-note theme, based on descending intervals of a major third, appears first in the opening movement at the words: 'Das Firmament blaut ewig.' The same figure is transformed in the 'Abschied', when the solo recitative is first heard; and from descending intervals of a major third, the main arches of the movement take their curve: ('Ich sehne mich, O Freund', and 'Die liebe Erde'.) All the best of Mahler is in this work, the naive poet, the cunning artist, the child and the man, and the gatherer of harvests and the sower of new seeds, the composer who brought the romantic movement in music to an end and also pointed the way to the immediate future. It was Mahler who directed Schönberg to new paths. The naive Mahler, with all his banality, was both the epigone and the prophet; he glanced back and he looked forward.

VII

The convenience of writers on Mahler would have been suited if he had died after the composition of 'Das Lied von der Erde'; here was the 'farewell', the leavetaking from the world, properly histrionic. But there was still the musician in Mahler to satisfy, the instrumental composer who had lost his way in the world of the symphony because he endeavoured to live in it to the full extent of his complex nature. When he wrote 'Das Lied von der Erde' he knew that after all he had created a masterpiece; harmony entered his soul for a while. Before he died, he needed to compose a wordless symphony, in which he might make his philosophy and valediction symphonic and universal, not personal and lyrical. The human voice and the word could at last be dispensed with and transcended surely; for his command of symphonic resources, for years masterly, could now be exercised easefully; no longer had he to fight a sense of fear or failure. In the Ninth Symphony there is a warm depth of harmony not to be found elsewhere in Mahler's music; the last movement is the nearest to the style of adagio he composed; the tone and the calm expansions of the phrases are of the essence of the adagio style. It is probably a tribute to his master, Bruckner; the movement is turned down from the main keys of the symphony, D minor and D major to D flat, ending in D flat. The symphony is long from the very nature of the material. We may, if we choose, think that Mahler's material in the Ninth Symphony is not interesting enough or put together arrestingly enough to cover the expansive canvas; but it is irrelevant to object to length and duration. A listener is free to tell a composer he doesn't like a 'long' work; the composer is also at liberty to retort that he doesn't like a listener with a short music-sense.

The material of the Ninth Symphony of Mahler is not inadequate for the spacious plan laid down in the first movement, which presses forward at once to the finale. The work, as a fact, is one of the most engrossing symphonies of the last half-century; the first movement is one of the greatest first movements since Beethoven's Ninth. I do not know a greater, not even the first movements of Brahms's First and Fourth. Out of the closing chord of the 'Das Lied von der Erde' the theme of this first movement is born. Mahler sums up the style and technique – the rationale – of first-movement form. After this movement, there was little left for other composers except to pour their material into the finally developed mould. The main and long opening theme or episode suggests a cradle-song which is enlarged gradually to a mature man's review of his life. Then the movement is transformed to a march macabre; the crisis at the section marked 'Mit höchster Gewalt', where there is a sudden pedal-point, with trombones and tuba sounding a summons, while a bass drum or tamtam beats a rhythm based on the movement's fundamental intervals, and muted trumpets blow mysterious fanfares – this passage has few equals in symphonic music as a moving and original expression of a last and braced-up facing of one's destiny. The whole movement, indeed, is an epilogue to a life lived for music. Mahler must, of course, write his own obituary. There is another magnificent stroke, when the trumpet motif – a Fate motif obviously – is resolved to the haunting horn melody which beckons to the sentimental coda, with the solo violin swooning its portamento in a misty nocturne of harp and flute: another and the very last example of the Mahler contradiction; the material is passé, but by his individual style and power of musical thought and feeling Mahler puts the coping-stone on the romantic and baroque symphonic edifice. In the second and third movements, especially in the rondo burlesco, he even approaches a mockery of his own curiously mixed bucolic and cosmopolitan flavours. Not often is the romantic gesture combined with Mahler's sharpness of intellect; the actor in him remained to the end.

Something is wrong with our critical values if we allow Mahler to drop into the limbo of things taken for granted, simply because at some time or other a phrase or label was applied to him during a momentary 'reaction'. I find him perpetually interesting as a problem of aesthetic psychology and as a maker of music.

VI

Strauss, the Tragic-Comedian
1864-1949

Strauss, the Tragic-Comedian

In the nineteenth century Pluto held sway over music as over most other things in his widening world. The art expanded beyond its old frontiers; domains of literature, even of painting, were plundered and annexed. Orchestras swelled like armies, and they threatened to become as heavy in accoutrement. Great opera houses and concert halls produced a strange breed of listener; the serried rows of boxes drooped with the weight and fatigue of millionaires eager for culture. A new music was wanted for a new public, a public that understood more – a little more – about literature than about music, though it was pursuing its studies in 'appreciation' industriously enough. So the symphonic-poem was gratefully seized upon; the story or programme could always be followed even when the thread of the musical discourse seemed to get entangled. Besides, the old symphonies scarcely gave the orchestra a chance; and this was the age of the orchestra. (Somebody even suggested the rewriting of Beethoven's trumpet parts.)

The time, the Zeitgeist, produced the man, as usual. In the appropriate atmosphere the genius of Richard Strauss flourished. We were all trying to read Nietzsche; and Strauss at once set him to music, and made our general culture much easier to assimilate, even if it must be admitted that we had to accustom ourselves to what the programme-analysts called his horizontal harmony. But he made a regular royal sound in the orchestra; and that is what we loved most of all. Then he wrote an opera which came home to nearly everybody in the multitudinous and bejewelled audiences of the period. The age was producing a natural cynicism. Gilda and Lucia were fading into museum-pieces. Charpentier's *Louise*, though in the fashionable vein of simulated realism – with the necessary juice of sentiment to wash it all down – unfortunately dealt with the working classes. *Der Rosenkavalier* was a masterstroke of opportunism. To sit in a brilliant opera house of those receding years, and to hear and see *Rosenkavalier* was to realize that opera and life were for once in a while matched perfectly. The audience, the stage-picture, all the fascinating dyes and odours of the music, were only as so many different aspects of the latest act in the eternal comedy of manners. For though Hofmannsthal placed his libretto in the rococo world of Maria Theresa, the music of Strauss belonged to our modern world. Though the niggerboy's flourish at the opera's end seemed to fix the sadness of the Marschallin's story in a distant past, Strauss was cunning and understood his public. The Marschallin was made real and close to us; many times, when I have attended this opera in the capital cities of the world, I have felt how intimate and pointed was the byplay between stage and many a private and darkened retreat in the theatre. Many a woman has heard her own heart speaking in the Marschallin's music. And all round have I felt the presence, in boxes and stalls, of many Oktavians and Sophies, young life at the springtime. Imagination has heard time running out like sand during performances of *Rosenkavalier* in a great opera house at the height of a season in the old days. Strauss, the sentimentalist, the cynic, the materialist, the composer who set the nineteenth century to music, to opulent music! He can be called all these things, but he cannot be called them with more force than he can be called a genius and the greatest story-teller in music the world has so far known.

He set the nineteenth century to music; a figure of

speech, but it will serve. Nearly every major work of
Strauss begins with great expansion of energy, a leaping
upwards; then follows a culmination of force, size and
intricacy of parts; then a descent into disillusionment or
futility. At the outset of *Don Juan* the music has a fine
athletic springiness; a trained-to-the-muscle propulsive
strength; the call of the four horns to action is grand and
thrilling; the sequences towards the climax are masterful
and proud and magnificent. The end is revulsion, dramatically necessary, of course, for the point of the poem; but
how convincingly Strauss does it! Not as convincingly does
he conclude *Heldenleben*, when a noble conclusion was
urgently demanded, after the hero's gigantic climbings in
the first section of the work, where we can almost see his
fist-shakings, his penultimate intake of energy before his
final capture of the summit. But the end is no heroic
apotheosis; the superman lapses into human-all-too-human
comforts; we cannot feel that a victory of the spirit has been
torn out of the storm. Again, in *Tod und Verklärung*, there
is no spiritual victory; the peroration is hollow and rhetorical. And the seven-leagued boots of Zarathustra are changed
in the finale of the symphonic-poem for the fireside slippers
of a tired man. Even *Der Rosenkavalier* ends with the
astringent jangling of the Silver Rose motif; disillusionment
is not far away.

Another strange point; Strauss's music seems to follow
the psychological curve of the nineteenth century, a curve
from urge and conquest to unfulfilment; also it traces the
main psychological curve of Strauss's own career as an
artist – from the brave dawn of *Don Juan* to the resigned
close. Let us look into this strange tragi-comedy. We need
not stress our moral tale; it will emerge as we proceed. As
Hazlitt said of Spenser's *Faerie Queene*, we need not be
afraid of the Allegory; it won't bite us.

II

The ironic imps made sport with Strauss from the beginning. They dressed him when he was young in the sober and discreet garb of the respected absolute musicians of the period. In the Violin Sonata, in the 'Burleske', and the Piano Quartet, his three most significant early works, Strauss's emerging genius assumes at times the aspect of Brahms. But mischief, and the bedevilment to come, peep out from under the cowl. Till Eulenspiegel flits through the Improvisation of the Violin Sonata, winks at Johannes during the middle part of the 'Burleske', and threatenes to disturb the academic decorum of the Quartet in the scherzo. At the age of twenty-four, Strauss plunged into the vortex of nineteenth-century music; he was his own Don Juan, sending his young eagles into the sun, dazzled with the urge and cleverness given him by his fates. Master of the orchestra at twenty-four, an orchestra of the age of gold and brass; here were riches and temptation, the orchestra of Midas. It is difficult even yet to believe that a young man composed *Don Juan*; it is the most remarkable example of music of genius springing full-armed into action. It is true that Mozart and Schubert showed their genius before they were twenty-four; but in 1884 the merely cerebral part of the labour of composition had developed to a length not dreamed of by Mozart, Schubert or Beethoven. The simple task of copying the instrumental parts of *Don Juan*, let alone thinking of them or organizing them, would have given poor Schubert the vertigo. The composing of *Don Juan* was one of the miracles of music; bliss it must have been for Strauss to be alive in that young dawn; nay, it was high noon for him before he knew that he *was* born, throwing masses of tone about him like a lord of creation, raising new worlds, whipping up whirlwinds of string-tone, then subduing them to a warm glow of brass and horn. Never before had violins cracked such a whip as Strauss cracked for the unleashing of *Don Juan*; he found with unerring instinct the right musical habitat for his theme. The whole point of *Don Juan* is that life must be a welter for the Don to plunge into recklessly. Where is there a welter of orchestration more reckless than the welter which Strauss sets into motion with one stroke at the beginning of *Don Juan*? Not until now had music known this heady, springy yet taut energy; music had, as Samuel Butler said, wriggled with Bach, and writhed with Wagner – extravagant language, no doubt, but we can see the point of it. Berlioz kept the body and muscles of music well trained, even to gauntness, while feeding the art on the romantic sweets. Then for years music languished in the drowsy air of hot voluptuous interiors. Strauss never was a romantic; he was made of sterner stuff, and, what is more, he was made of worldly stuff. There is no nostalgia in Strauss; whenever he glances back, it is without ache. The Marschallin sings of time that stealthily steals beauty from life. But Strauss uses time purely and simply as a dramatic effect perceived by an artist conniving objectively a picture, a pattern; he uses time ironically not poetically. No; Strauss has always been too objective, too much the sharp realistic observer, to fit in with a romantic aesthetic which asks for a certain reflectiveness, a sense of the pathos of distance. Strauss tells the tale of Eulenspiegel without either sentimentality doting on the past or on legendary characters; he rounds off his narrative with a perfect little epilogue which says, without moralizing and without romantic regret: 'It all happened so long ago'; it is a sort of chimney-corner ending as the children release their pent-up breath.

In *Don Juan*, Strauss is not only a narrator; he is the life-force and protagonist. I cannot think that this work was

composed at a writing-table by a young man sitting apart
from what he was hurling into existence; I see him hurled
with it, for a lifetime, until weary and spent.

The new toy tyrannized him. A bigger orchestra, a
mightier world to conquer every time. Temporary defeat
occurred when he invaded the territory of idealism and
religiosity and forgot to take with him his irony. Later in
life he learned to know better; for he wrote a letter to
Hofmannsthal confessing that the *Josephslegende* was beyond him, as there was no piety at all in the Strauss family.
Tod und Verklärung is the most subjective of the tone-
poems of Strauss – and herein rests a tale of some importance to our discussion of his aesthetic and psychological
make-up. The most objective of the tone-poems is *Till
Eulenspiegel*; it is an etching of Till seen from the outside.
Strauss does not let the rascal dawdle and dream, and he
does not, as I say, moralize. *Till Eulenspiegel* bites into the
mind like the lines of a medieval woodcut. The use in this
work of rondo-form was an inspiration; the first condition of
the grotesque style is a contracted energy which turns upon
itself in lines of black and white. Despite the clamour of
orchestration in *Till*, the scoring is not fulsome in a slowly
expanding harmony, as in *Tod und Verklärung*. Strauss is
at his best when he sees swiftly and objectively; he is at
his worst when he trusts to subjective emotion and to the
deliberate and spacious harmonic rhetoric of the German
romantic school proper. *Tod und Verklärung* is a failure
because in it Strauss attempted to treat a spiritual idea in the
style of Lisztian 'transcendentalism'. This symphonic-poem
conforms to the broad and gradually modulated sequences
of a slow movement, a development-section of quick tempi,
and a resolution of dissonance into the Lisztian apotheosis.
But Strauss could not make music at this slow-moving pace;
as soon as he stops to think or to feel he lapses into the banal.

Tod und Verklärung is vivid enough when Strauss is describing the airless stillness of the sick-room, the slipping away of life, the wan flickerings of the rushlight, the terrible suspense, the failing heartbeats. When we reach the trailing clouds of glory of childhood, and the transfiguration to loftier spheres, the music echoes the cadence which denotes the ending of the perfect day, or the Serenata of Braga. Strauss has neither ethic nor metaphysic, neither romance nor reflection. He writes illustrated fiction in music; he changes Nietzsche's *Zarathustra* into a novel of adventure. We do not think of his works, even of the purely instrumental works, in terms of music; his art is graphic, and when the sounds of the Straussian orchestra have died down, as today they seem to be dying down like an ebbing sea, our imagination is left alive with pictures: Till, jaunty with hands in pockets walking away whistling; Till, upsetting academic apple-carts, skyrocketing and somersaulting, riding the broomstick of mischief; Till, before the judges, disrespectful and not entirely subdued; Till, hitched aloft by the rope, squeaking out his last breath, then dangling like a puppet of rag and sawdust in the air. We see rather than hear Sancho Panza and Don Quixote shaking the water from their drenched bodies after the escapade in the boat; the pizzicato notes are the dripping of the water. We see rather than hear them kneel down and offer up their prayer of thanksgiving. We see rather than hear Salome's life battered out brutally, long after the curtain has fallen and the visual presentation has passed from memory. We see rather than hear the accumulation of hate and evil in *Elektra*, as Strauss's polyphony breeds and spreads like a cancer of music. We see rather than hear the Prince in *Die Frau ohne Schatten* turning to stone as the gongs are struck to a hardness that offends against all that music subsists on. We see rather than hear the bucolic gemütlich shape of Dulcinea; we see as well as we hear the panniered sweep of the Marschallin when she enters and commands the stage in Act III of *Rosenkavalier*; we see as well as we hear the Hero's Consort wheedling the hero in *Heldenleben*. We do not indeed always *hear* the music in our minds as we see these creations of Strauss; with other composers of programme-music or opera, nothing remains for imagination to seize on if we forget the actual thematic and musical stuff of their presentations. Strauss at times seemed ready to barter the very ears of music in exchange for more and more eyes. In the nineteenth century, which witnessed the evolution of the camera to the cinema, Strauss gave us the first motion pictures – in music, with the appropriate 'fade-outs'. What are the closing scenes of *Don Quixote* and *Heldenleben* but perfectly calculated and lighted 'fade-outs'?

III

Heldenleben is a self-portrait with a closeness of detail rare in music, seen from the outside, composed much as a man takes his own photograph in a room. There is no subjective or internal revelation, such as Tchaikovsky gives us in the Fourth Symphony and the 'Pathétique'. Strauss himself has stated that *Heldenleben* does not depict a heroism of everyday life, 'but rather a heroism that corresponds to the inward battle of life which aspires through efforts and renunciation towards the elevation of the soul'. The work gives the lie to this highfalutin' and heavily German statement. The energy of the themes; the rapid changes of scene; the episodic form; the imitation, or, so to say, musical onomatopoeia – you do not universalize ideas and emotions by devices as graphic and dynamic as these. *Heldenleben* is an exciting panorama of adventures in music

and orchestration; nothing more and nothing less. Dr
Johnson said that a man might as well hang himself as look
for a story in the novels of Samuel Richardson; a man
might as well hang himself as look for anything apart from
a story in Strauss.

Strauss, a successor to Wagner, Liszt and Berlioz? – on
the contrary, he was the first of the composers to provide a
corrective to the full-blown romanticism of the great line of
Weber, Schubert, Wagner, Schumann, Liszt and Berlioz.
This style of romanticism was remote from the new world
of nineteenth-century 'discovery' and 'progress'. Strauss
brought music out of remote realms; for him the proper
study of mankind was man, and of course, woman. He
planted music on the earth of his own times. Strauss is
always a contemporary, even when he is dealing with
legend or history, which he re-creates or restores with the
newest 'sets' and costumes from his orchestral wardrobe.
The most vital note in his music is an astringent criticism
of life bred by contact with the visible universe. When he
does, at times, venture a height of idealism, the aspiration
is not Wagnerian or Lisztian; it does not involve a renunciation of the world, the flesh and the devil – at least not for
long. The idea of redemption as a theme for musical
treatment became almost a trick of the composer's trade in
Germany. It actually controlled form and method of
harmonic transition. Strauss in *Heldenleben* achieves not
renunciation but exhaustion; the battle is, like all battles,
without a lasting peace. He seeks convalescence not in
idealism but in isolation. He reviews his life as an artist, in
a dexterous tissue of polyphony that weaves reminiscences
from his own works. It is like a thematic catalogue played
in public. To the end, Strauss's Hero remains of the earth.
And he tastes the dust of disillusion. Sentimentality
inevitably steals in. Strauss has never written a long slow

movement of fibre; his active genius flowed into mutable episodic forms – rondo, variation, pastiche. He has rushed here and there with his camera of music, ever curious and restless, ranging through the great and the little world, seldom finding the fulfilled moment when, like Faust, he could say:

Verweile doch, du bist so schön!

The theme that sketches the superman of Strauss's early ambition, in *Heldenleben* is, with all its arrogance and tenacity, susceptible to sudden fallings and subsidences, hinting at some essential weakness of the spirit. The Hero is as easily depressed as he is exalted. He moans like a beast in pain, in the trombones and tubas. A pathos emerges of which maybe Strauss was not conscious; self-revelation by chance and not aware of what it is telling us. The 'Adversaries' are exposed not as inimical fates and forces; they are – bless us! – musical critics, baldpates and eunuchs, or merely obese. Then the Consort cajoles our Hero. This is remarkable illustrative music; the solo violin plays a cadenza which, plain as plain, caresses the superman, who is clearly feeling sorry for himself. She teases him; the violin's recitative is unmistakable. 'And did they say his music was ugly then?' She comforts him from behind the cushioned chair into which he has disgustedly flung himself. At first he grumpily rejects her common sense and her banter; the tuba and trombones turn away from her, sulky with the sense of being hopelessly misunderstood. Then, at last, they raise up the Hero once more; he is refreshed; he is restored to his vain self and the banner of his ego is unfurled again. Strauss tells us all this in apt terms. The miracle is that *qua* music the passage is satisfying enough. But where is Strauss's abstract or generalized heroism? If this portrait is not intimate and particular; if Strauss attempted a loftier and

more universal kind of music, what was he thinking about
to speak here with such precision and intimacy of mortal
weaknesses and foibles?

The reader, I hope, has not misunderstood my argument,
as it has proceeded so far. I am not unduly deploring Strauss's
want of that idealism which inspired the main style of
orchestral music from Beethoven onwards for a hundred
years. After Wotan, Ochs was a distinct and refreshing
change; after the Ninth Symphony the approachable world
of Till and Don Quixote was a revolt and holiday from awe.
It is not the task of criticism to estimate artists according
to ethical values. Beethoven and Bach were greater than
Strauss because they were the greater musical geniuses. I
doubt if a composer's ethic or his aesthetic matters very
much if he is inventive, if his musical ideas are strong,
fruitful and original.

The theory or notion still circulates that Strauss corrupted
his genius through his traffickings with programme-music;
that no composer can hope to create masterpieces if he aims
at illustration and portraiture. Music, we are told, cannot
express definite emotions, or refer in any way to the visible
and external universe. Without the key or clue of the
written programme, we are further told, we should not
know what the music of *Till Eulenspiegel* was saying. For
that matter we should not know what any language was
saying except for its association-values. A foreigner needs to
consult a dictionary if he does not know what an English
word means. In other words, he has to consult the programme. 'Death' is a terrible and beautiful word if you
have grown up with its association-values: 'Tod' is as vivid
to a German and stupid to the majority of English folk. All
language, musical or other, is ideographic; I mean that it
conveys significances only because its elements, its parts of
speech, have been linked for long years with certain ideas or

sets of feeling – arbitrarily linked at that; for really there is no reason why instead of one sound or arrangement of letters to denote an idea or set of feelings, another sound or arrangement of letters should not have been used. Only the crudest onomatopoeic utterances convey a meaning that does not depend on a definition or 'programme'. Why, then, should music have put aside at any time the enrichment in significance that comes from association-values? As well might the human race have insisted that language remained 'absolute', that is, onomatopoeic.

Upon this question of absolute and programme-music much confusion of thought has occurred, even in the minds of great composers. Beethoven, for example, felt that he needed to apologize for the 'Pastoral' Symphony. He bluffed himself that the music was 'mehr Empfinding als Malerei'; more feeling than painting; yet he introduced into the work descriptive touches as imitative as any in Strauss. His storm, we can well believe, would have achieved as bold a discordance as that of the battle-section in *Heldenleben* if the orchestra of Beethoven's period had been capable of a Straussian riot and clangour of tone. Beethoven felt no compunction about writing at the beginning of the finale of the Ninth Symphony a stretch of recitative which is entirely alien to the self-contained style of absolute music. If Beethoven had offered us this recitative as pure music he would have exposed himself to the charge of musical ineptitude. No composer would write such a passage from a strict musical intention; Beethoven's declamatory double-basses are expressing an extra-musical idea. In other words, they are guilty of 'programme-music'. Imagine these sounds in a Mozart symphony....

So with the high-priest of the absolutists – Brahms. He begins the fourth movement of his C minor Symphony with a stretch of pizzicato which in an absolute pattern of music could not hope to find justification for being there at all. Brahms is obviously expressing some idea or feeling that defied expression in any sequence of notes of absolute music. We can imagine the raised eyebrows of a Mozart if these ominous plucked notes had fallen upon his ear as he listened to a symphony of a composer who was supposed to be defending pure music from the impure. 'Heavens, the man does not know how to write satisfyingly to the musical ear, else why make such odd and irregular sounds?' But Mozart, being a dramatist in music, would surely have added: 'He's telling us a story of some sort.'

Brahms and Beethoven, it seems, are at liberty to write programme-music in a symphony; but Strauss, because he openly writes it and calls a spade a spade, and gives us a clue, is suspect of sinning against the true nature or function of music. 'Ah but', say the pure in heart, 'Beethoven and Brahms express emotion in the abstract; Strauss expresses concrete things, even tries to imitate sounds of the physical universe.' The irony of the argument is that music in its virgin beginnings probably expressed nothing *but* sounds of the physical universe – echoes of rustling leaves, or rippling waters. Only by long association with emotion and ideas did music come to acquire its power to convey any sort of appeal to man's mind and feelings. For the life of me I cannot see why Beethoven is composing 'legitimate' music when he describes or suggests a struggle with fate; and why Strauss is giving us 'illegitimate' music when he describes or suggests a battle with his adversaries. We are dealing here, surely, not with a difference of kind, but a difference of degree; Beethoven composes the better of the two men simply because his mind is the more consistently musical. The emotional or conceptual starting point of both composers is related, not antithetical. The real difference is that Beethoven approximates to epic poetry, and Strauss to

141

narrative. In poetry and literature we do not reject a Walter Scott because he is not a Milton; then why deny Strauss his unique gifts as a story-teller in music? If and when he fails, the cause is not an abuse of the 'nature' of music; the breakdown comes from a weakening of musical inspiration.

IV

The trouble with music is that the virgin Saint Cecilia presides over it; music somehow obtained the name of the divine art, the art to which in heaven all the cherubim and the morning stars of creation devote themselves. At the time of the rising of Strauss's comet the conviction was firmly held amongst many musicians in England and Europe that if a composer chose to set a Biblical text in the form of an oratorio, tongues of fire and the dove would from sheer habit descend and touch his brow. Strauss came into all this hocus-pocus like his own Till, turning catherine-wheels of string tone, skimming urchin-slides of trumpet brilliance over the thin ice of rondo-form; and squeaking abuse from bassoons and oboes; gurgling obscenely in bass clarinets; belching in brass and tuba. 'Shall we rouse the night owl in a catch?' Malvolio was awakened in the nightdress of pure music. And Strauss whirls his wind-machine; and antic parabola in his orchestra asks: 'Dost thou think because thou art virtuous there shall be no more cakes and ale?'

In the passing of time we may learn how sick of self-love, of self-pity, was the art of Europe in the years when the young pagan Strauss raised his aureoled head. Music was bleeding to death of the wound of Amfortas; Nietzsche longed for the lost gay science, the dancing and singing muse. As Schopenhauer spoke his luscious mantled pessimism through Wagner, so did Nietzsche speak through Strauss. Even the banality of the waltz of Zarathustra, in Strauss's tone-poem, was the gesture of a refreshing irresponsibility in an art which for years had apparently lived long on cold heights of the Christian ethic. It is the complaint of Strauss's critics that he always lacked taste. 'Strauss was never the fine, the perfect artist,' writes Paul Rosenfeld in his brilliant set of studies called *Musical Portraits*, 'even in the first flare of youth, even at the time when he was the meteoric dazzling figure flaunting over all the baldpates of the universe ... it was apparent that there were serious flaws in his spirit.' Of course Strauss has lacked taste: could he have corrected solemnity had he been fastidious? Bach in his organ loft; Handel seeing God (but slyly substituting pagan melodies in the 'Messiah' with the accommodating faith of his generation); Brahms for a while walking with peas in his boots the path of affliction, supporting his cross of pedal-points and double-fugues; César Franck anointing himself with his own unguents of chromaticism; Mahler selling his Judaism for a mess of sensuous Catholicism in his 'Veni Creator' Symphony; Bruckner watching and praying through the eternity of *his* 'Nine' – it was high time that music was brought down to earth. Strauss, in *Heldenleben*, seeks inspiration from man's common clay; from the teeming earth; from great upspringing cities. The pace is too quick to last, maybe; none the less the exercise did the art of music a world of good; much adipose tissue was lost. Music was given a cold bath by Strauss; the harmonic slime laid on by years of chromaticism was washed away. It was Strauss, after all, who turned the attention of orchestral music once again to polyphony, to incisive lines, after the confinement in walls of block harmony. One of the several ironies in the life and career of this tragic-comedian Strauss, is that in the end he suffered a fate not at all uncommon amongst the athletic fraternity; he himself developed adiposity and nearly died of fatty degeneracy of orchestration. The age's fatal disease and elephantiasis claimed him. But though the *Zeitgeist* made him and nearly ruined him, he was spared one of its scourges; he never suffered self-righteousness. He lived and died a pagan.

V

Strauss, of course, has his enigma. Like every great genius, he was a full man and we must take him as we find him, with the elements in him strangely mixed. He never satisfied his disciples, never conformed to a clique, was never consistent enough in aim or style to encourage a movement. The superman one year; man of this fleshly world next year; and then he puts on his slippers and calls the children to the fireside while he tells the tale of Don Quixote. The Hero turned uncle; Zarathustra married, in velvet jacket, wiping his feet on the doormat before venturing into his own house, as Deems Taylor has told us. I saw him at Salzburg several years ago, pink-cheeked and genial, performing a little fandango in the empty street at midnight outside the Oestreichischeshof; his companion was Clemens Kraus; that evening there had been a splendid performance of *Die Frau ohne Schatten* at which I had seen Strauss applauding delightedly and crying out at the end: 'Bravo! Bravo!' He described this opera to me as a 'Meisterwerk'. 'At last,' he said, 'I have learned how to score.' He made this extraordinary statement without boastfulness; indeed, he implied that his works so far, *Till*, *Rosenkavalier*, *Ariadne*, *Don Quixote*, had been mere 'prentice work in orchestration. His faults are not always the faults of worldliness. In 1895, when he composed *Zarathustra*, the

Straussites hailed a new dawn for music. 'Here', they said, echoing Nietzsche, is 'the prelude to a deeper, mightier, perchance a more evil and mysterious music; a German music that does not fade wither and die away beside the blue and wanton sea and the clear Mediterranean sky'. The Straussites saw only the shooting ray of trumpet tone that announces the sunrise in *Also Sprach Zarathustra*; they had no ears for the gemütlich *tempo di valse* to which the super-man danced in his carpet slippers. And next year, in 1896, he composed *Don Quixote*; calling children to the chimney-corner and holding them there.

The Straussians, of course, missed the point of the work. This, they averred, was a study of Don Quixote, deeper than ever Cervantes could go, a penetration in the light of 'modern' psychology. The new symphonic-poem had some-how to be got into the canon, bleating sheep, windmills and all, alongside *Zarathustra* and *Tod und Verklärung*. We can see today that *Don Quixote* is purely and simply a tale told over again in music; Strauss dwells affectionately on some story book of his childhood, with woodcuts. I once possessed such a book, and never do I hear *Don Quixote* without seeing the old engravings again and getting a sense of the faded paper. For the remarkable fact about *Don Quixote* is that in spite of the numerous instrumental forces demanded by the score, Strauss never wrote music clearer in texture than here. With his customary instinct he found the right musical idiom for his theme; the thick texture of *Tod und Verklärung* or the whip-crack energies of *Don Juan*, would have been ruinous to the subject of the adventures of Cervantes' crazy knight and Sancho Panza. The point of the work is that Strauss does nothing more than amuse himself by translating the main and most pictorial episodes of the novel into music. There is hardly a hint of commentary from Strauss himself, except at the very end, as

I shall presently show; there is certainly no psychologizing or philosophizing. Strauss simply narrates to us, in the language of music, chapters from Cervantes – trying to be as objective and as true to the original as Florian was in *his* translation. Strauss invariably found not only the right musical idiom for his themes or programmes; also he found the right form. The rondo, as we have seen, was clearly the only musical form in which to express Till's somersaulting and persistent escapades; as naturally did the adventures of Don Quixote and the mutations of his distorted visions call for variation form. And the choice of the 'cello for a delineation of Don Quixote in music was an inspiration; the very shape of the 'cello, the colour of the wood, as well as the tone, seems to me by some subtle law of association to evoke the visage of the Knight of the Rueful Countenance.

Nothing in Strauss is happier or closer to genius than the aptness of the chivalry themes: they have a poised and prancing sort of lilt and pride which appeals to the imagination at times like a Bayeux tapestry of music. During the opening section, where the Knight is in his study fuddling his brains with the old lore of tourney, Strauss allures us into seeing, through a haze of years as well as through the pathetic maze of the poor unbalanced mind, flashes of rearing horses, calls of trumpet and clash of lance. And the great thing is that Strauss does not allow the madness of *Don Quixote* to harden, as in music it might easily have hardened, to the style of musical grotesque; Strauss keeps Don Quixote as human, and as sweet and lovable, as Cervantes. The characterization of Sancho Panza is as unfaltering in touch, and as wonderfully apposite, in musical style. There is no passage, even in Strauss, where music *talks* as plainly to us as when Sancho, in the third variation, deals out worldly wisdom and the common sense of the countryman; here is the perfect musical apophthegm, and most humorously does Strauss flavour the accents with the smack of self-satisfied platitude.

We take our music with a heavy solemnity if we cannot laugh with Strauss in this work, where he is so ready to laugh himself. His bleating sheep episode has been relegated to the outer darkness – crude 'realism', unmusical etcetera, etcetera. But it is just a joke; moreover, it is one of music's best jokes. As an expression of mutton-headed stupidity, with the right herded immobility and vacancy of eye, this passage is sublimely comic. Yet it is usually laughed at surreptitiously by those who find it funny at all; it is as though we were to retire behind closed doors to read *Pickwick*. Strauss in *Don Quixote* empties the entire contents of his orchestral box of tricks for our delight; he whirls the windmill round and round, while the Knight attacks, with poor Sancho making the most agitated and appealing protests. He radiates arpeggios of childlike enchantment in the episode of the boat; and he lets Don Quixote die at last to a gorgeous sigh and slither down the 'cello, a trick that no composer would have dared to use if he had really grown up and achieved sophistication. In this symphonic-poem Strauss escaped for a while from his role and destiny; but the writing was now beginning to appear on the wall. The pretty postlude to *Don Quixote* is a regretful leave-taking from an intimate and fine-spun tale in music. Once again, though, a few years later, Strauss put on his carpet-slippers and velvet jacket in the *Sinfonia Domestica*, a work which has been curiously underrated even by admirers of Strauss, a work about which the critics have generally written pompously, presumably because the composer baths the baby and employs a huge orchestra; as a fact he employs it with geniality and gusto – and here and there with a masterful restraint. It was while discussing the *Sinfonia Domestica* that Ernest Newman described Strauss as a man of talent who had once been a man of genius. But the gods had not yet finished their sport with Strauss.

Not much more than a year after the composition of the comfortable bourgeois sentiment of the *Sinfonia Domestica*, Strauss staggered the world of music with *Salome*, and not much more than a year after that, he hurled *Elektra* at us, an eruption as though from a forgotten volcano. Here was a new style of orchestration and vocal writing; magnitude was galvanized out of sluggishness by whips of simulated hate, perversity of passion and brutality. It was, of course, not genuine; none the less, the diabolical cleverness of Strauss deceived us for just as long as our ears remained unaccustomed to its clashes of consonant and dissonant harmonies; and unaccustomed also to an orchestra which in *Salome* seemed to hiss and pursue the stage action like a fury crowned with snakes; and so long as we remained unaccustomed to the alternating polyphony of *Elektra* and its violence of harmony, which at one moment suggested a cancerous spreading of evil throughout the body of music, and then in its accumulation of massive weight filled the mind with visions of gruesome, maimed archaic limbs. But in both operas the growing cynicism of Strauss comes out in banalities of three-four time; the 'recognition' scene in *Elektra* and the 'Say au revoir but not goodbye' cadences of the closing scene of *Salome* could scarcely have passed the self-criticism of an artist wholly serious. Strauss, by these two 'shockers', drove the fashionable opera realism out of the hunt; the puny 'Veristi', with their diminutive 'Cavs.' and 'Pags.', could not stand against the gigantic machine of Strauss. Once again, and almost for the last time, Strauss served well the greedy, ruthless and devouring Time Spirit.

The reaction set in at last against neuroticism, sensualism and, as Sorin says, 'all the rest of it'. The Straussian genius for characterization and realism could be blended nicely

with quaintness, colour and old receding aromas of the
past: the chevalieresque style of *Don Quixote*, the verve
and racket of *Till*, the ardour of *Don Juan*, if it could be
recaptured; the devoutness of *Morgen* – why here was
Rosenkavalier waiting to be, so to say, assembled in all its
parts. The unction of Sancho Panza could be laid on with a
bolder trowel for Ochs. And the old trick of 'Once upon a
time', infallible in *Till Eulenspiegel* and *Don Quixote*,
could be exploited to bring down the curtain of the new
comedy for music with the niggerboy trotting here and
there looking for the handkerchief, to the music of his first
entrance into the opera. No wonder that Strauss sometimes
was composing the music of *Rosenkavalier* before Hofmannsthal had written the words or even arranged a scene
and incident-sequence. It is a ravishing work, in spite of
the restlessness of the orchestra, which can never stop
pointing and staring at the characters. It is a mirror of an
orchestra that flashes back the action to the stage – not
Debussy's mirror that captures and holds all images of the
visible world in a glass of enchantment. The Marschallin
enters the restaurant in the third act, and the orchestra
swells to a panniere of tone, so that the rough accents and
phrases of Ochs himself change and broaden to graciousness.
When Sophie and Oktavian sit down, after the duet in Act
II, and begin polite conversation under the eye of the
Duenna, the orchestra at once engages in a perfect tête-à-
tête of swaying interchanging phrases. It is entrancing; and
is only one of a hundred such felicities in the best of all
entertainments presented for the delectation of civilized
men and women of all ages who go to opera. And Strauss
and Hofmannsthal allow gentle shadows to fall from time
to time upon the variegated scene, not only during
the obviously calculated episodes between Oktavian and the
Marschallin: a more artful touch is at the height of the

brilliant scene of the Marschallin's levée, when she gently chides her hairdresser: 'You have made me look middle-aged'. And the orchestra's flutes flash and ripple with the hairdresser's swiftly moving fingers. Even an indiscretion of one of the lap-dogs shown to the Marschallin by the animal-vendor does not escape the absorbing eye of Strauss's kaleidoscope of orchestration.

Der Rosenkavalier marked the beginning of the end. 'Wo war ich schon einmal' sings Oktavian. The curtain falls to the tinklings of the 'Silver Rose' motif, brittle and bitter-sweet. With the curtain and the gesture of the brocaded niggerboy, Strauss also receded into the past. The Zeitgeist had finished with him; the rebel of yesterday was now the conservative of the present. *Ariadne* is a comparatively light-fingered, light-textured score, at times as finely musical as any Strauss had composed so far; but the realms of classic antiquity and of eighteenth-century wit and decorative irony end in a Teutonically accented pastiche.

There is much superb music in *Die Frau ohne Schatten*, and Strauss still throws his orchestral colour about and stains his tissue of tone with the dyes of Barak. It is indeed the most elaborate of the Strauss–Hofmannsthal operas. To no other of their productions did the two men bring as much thought, loftiness of purpose, and hard experienced labour as to *Die Frau ohne Schatten*.

Only a German-Austrian feeling for symbolism and apotheosis could have conceived and shaped this music-drama, which mingles abnormally the remote and inimically magical and the pathetically trustful human. It is all very un-English, no doubt. But the fact remains, the work occupied the minds of two men of genius, each a flower of his particular civilization. It possessed them intellectually and imaginatively. With the wreckage of a world war about them they found in their absorption in *Die Frau* fortitude and idealism. In a world shipwrecked Strauss forgot the world for a while. This opera was not put together mainly for the entertainment of the crowd but as a way of grasping at life as spirit and material manifestation of spirit. It is a sort of Weltanschauung, possibly confused in parts and liable to appear pretentious here and there to English common sense, but none the less to be taken into serious account. It may be hard for an English mentality to respond to *Die Frau*, but not harder, surely, than it is for a German or Austrian mentality to feel comfortable in the presence of, say, *Peter Grimes* or *The Turn of the Screw*.

Strauss was impelled to find a new style for this great libretto, vocally and orchestrally. The chief flaws or short-circuits in the score arise from the crowded, variegated, concentrated yet multifarious nature of Hofmannsthal's libretto. The imaginative worlds of it are terrestrial and superterrestrial; Hofmannsthal himself described the scope and welter of it: 'a fairy tale, in which two men and two women are set into contrast and conflict, one of the women fey and fairy, the other of the earth, yet though capricious good at heart; these characters encompassed by palace and humble home, priests, ships, rocks ...' but the summary loses grandeur and multifariousness expressed in English. Let the German give us the proper measure: 'Ein Zauber-märchen, worin zwei Männer und zwei Frauen einander gegenüberstehen ... die eine ein Feenwesen, die andere, irdirische, eine bizarre Frau mit einer guten Seele im Grunde, unbegreiflich launisch, herrisch und dabei doch sympathisch ... und das Ganze bunt, Palast, und Hütte, Priester, Fackeln, Felsengänge, Chöre, Kinder, das Ganze schwebt mir wirklich mit Gewalt vor Augen.' Even this grandiose inventory leaves out the grotesque, almost macabre Nurse, and the human-all-too-human Barak. To set the poem with no note or waste or any makeshift, a composer would need to mingle in himself the genius of Strauss, Debussy, Britten and Wolf. At times Hofmannsthal asks for a non-German atmosphere and swiftness of musical diction, and occasionally Strauss no doubt lapses into the orchestral language habitual to him at the time of the composition of *Die Frau*. There are one or two atavistic reachings back to the Wagner formulae. Not many, though. The astonishing thing is not that Strauss fails to integrate musically all of Hofmannsthal's material but that he comes so close to a clinching synthesis. Even in the closing scene, a spiritual apotheosis, in which the exalted tones of the redeemed are heard against a heavenly choir of children, Strauss by power of his technical mastery and his knowledge of every musical synonym, actually rises to the height of a lofty unearthly conception; and if at the end we are left with the feeling that we have been overwhelmed finally by a tour de force none the less we are compelled to admit that the enormous edifice of the work, as a whole, has been given a coping-stone of no slight weight with more than the hint of a wreath on it.

But in *Die Aegyptische Helena* he is without a new idea; the scoring seems bored with its own ingenuity. The opera is a hash of mysticism, pseudo-antique and spectacular, a sort of nightmare suffered after a champagne supper followed by a perusal of Lemprière as a bed-book. *Arabella* audaciously challenged comparisons with *Rosenkavalier*; we cannot but admire the nerve of the seventy-year-old Strauss who brought down the curtain on Act I of his latest opera with Arabella engaged in a soliloquy. Graf Waldner is half-brother to Ochs, and in the end Strauss was once again audacious; for he recalled the closing scene of *Rosenkavalier*, and proved that in 1933 he was still the only composer living who could compose a Strauss opera. *Daphne*, even more than *Arabella*, was a well-remembered work; it is like the supplementary index given away with an encyclopaedia; it is an outline of Strauss for those who have no time to study him in bulk.

Like his own Hero he heard at the decline of his powers ironical echoes of his own works, reminiscences from brave and burgeoning years. It is a commonplace of criticism to say that Strauss was the false dawn of modern music. On the contrary he was a sunset, an afterglow of Liszt and Wagner. Like Mr Polly, I happen to be fond of sunsets. Strauss was a genius, greater as a musician and an artist than as a man. It may be that, like Spontini, he was a composer for a particular period; it may be that several of his works amongst the symphonic-poems will seem in the eyes of posterity as so many remote lowly organized un-wieldy shapes, pterodactyls of music. But by his mistakes, as well as by his conquests, he closed an important chapter in the development of the art; he marked once for all the boundaries of programme-music. Only great men end epochs, as Mr Newman has said. Strauss sharpened the vocal style of opera; he quickened the vision and pulse of the orchestra. He tinctured romanticism with worldliness; he made brutality and realism vibrant and sensuous and attractive. He sinned against the divinity of the art; Wagner ravished music but Strauss raped her. Could any man not born a genius have given us *Till Eulenspiegel*, *Don Quixote*, *Elektra*, *Salome*, *Ariadne* and *Rosenkavalier*, not to mention 'Morgen', one of the world's most original and hauntingly lovely songs? Those of us who lived through the years of Strauss's rise to undisputed if brief leadership of music; those of us who experienced the excitement of his orchestra of many tongues and colours; those of us who experienced the first rapture and intoxication of Strauss's music, will not expect in one and the same lifetime to know the like of it again. No composer since Strauss has swept the world and walked through music with the stride of a Colossus, making dwarfs of his contemporaries.

He made, after all, a good end; the last phase might even be called 'Strauss und Verklärung'. In the 'Vier letzte Lieder' his music became mellow and entirely sensitive as he made a resigned farewell to life full of good memories, with no regrets. The vocal line of these songs is often fine-spun in its floating ornaments; yet ornament is the wrong word, as it might suggest expression that is self-conscious or given to display: The melisma of 'Frühling', the impulse of every fluttering turn or gush of notes, come from a pure musical response to the poem. 'Im Abendrot' and 'Beim Schlafengehen' Strauss arrives at his ripest mingling of significant song-speech and full-throated lyrical curve. The beginning of 'Beim Schlafengehen' at the words 'Nun der Tag mich müd' gemacht', and so on, is absolutely apt note after note, as each word of the beautiful poem of Hermann Hesse is set; for example, the rising semiquavers to 'Sehnliches' and the interval drop on 'freundlich', with the semiquaver pause. These settings abound in such felicities, all unself-consciously put down. Strauss at last is fulfilled and ready to depart, as the autumn surrounds him and the sun goes down. There is nothing in Strauss more genuine, more truly heart-opening, more warmly and more eloquently musical than the crescendo in 'Im Abendrot' at the line 'So tief im Abendrot', with the descent of strings and wood-wind into beautiful horn and trombone harmonies. The quotation from *Tod und Verklärung* at the words, marvellously intoned, 'ist dies etwa der Tod?' is unforced and steals in inevitably as memory. In this setting, especially, the mingling of speech and song, or rather of poetic vocal utterance with musical tone and shape, is of the finest art and sensibility. I need quote only the opening phrase, after an introduction of harvested and flowing orchestral bounty: 'Wir sind durch Not und Freude gegangen Hand in Hand.' In these songs we have a distillation of Strauss, the essence, orchestrally and vocally. So in the closing scene of *Capriccio*, where Madeleine sings of the two fires between which her heart burns; here is the Strauss crescendo and change of tonality in excelsis, enriched by a lifetime of art and experience of the world. After Strauss's sun had set, the afterglow was rich and consummatory.

VII

César Franck
1822–1890

César Franck

The world of music at times unfolds itself to the fancy in the shapes and altitudes of the physical universe. There, in the upper ether, reposes the mountain of Bach; farther away in a fiercer light the peak of Palestrina pierces the heavens like a spear; in a middle height the warmth of a more humane air makes fertile the slopes of the Handel range; the volcano of Beethoven smokes ominously yet, but there are wooded uplands enriched for ever by the lava of the first eruption. The enchanted lake of Debussy dreams in the distance; there are the courts and palaces and lawns of Mozart; there is the country estate of Haydn; there are rocks and crags and thunder to the right, where the Wagnerian surge is never still. And standing aloof, rising from a plateau, is the cathedral of César Franck.

Before our metaphor grows unwieldy let us drop it and consider César Franck as an example of musical Gothic. He has been called the father of modern French music; he would need unusual wisdom to recognize his own children. The tough tissue of the Walloon stock was in him, as in Beethoven; for this reason he got no closer to a French school than Beethoven to the Viennese school. Franck as a teacher inspired every musician of France who came into his presence; but we are engaged here in defining and appreciating his own style. French music, as far as it can be discussed with any relevance to Franck, has certain unmistakable points. Sensibility rather than imagination is the main source. In Franck there is much less of sensibility than imagination. Sensibility insists on a fastidious technique of expression; Franck is seldom fastidious. The French school, since Franck, has cultivated the picturesque and the decorative, and has aimed more at precision than at musical fullness or sonority. Franck is never picturesque at his truest; he is devout not decorative; piety and not aestheticism is his inspiration. His music reflects nothing of the literary influences which at all times have more or less governed French composers; in fact Franck's finest work is the only 'absolute' music ever written by a composer in any way merged into a French musical tradition. I leave out of account the eclectic Saint-Saëns, who was *capable de tout*. But the main characteristic of Franck, one which I think excludes him from the widest canon of French music, is his genius for the grotesque. He could compose a scherzo – and what other French composer has done that? I do not forget the 'Queen Mab' Scherzo of Berlioz, a dance of picturesque fancy, in no way related to the demonism of the grotesque style, which since Beethoven has been the essence of the scherzo. Franck belongs to a musical architecture definitely Gothic and romantic grotesque. There is no demonism in French music; the diablerie of Berlioz is a dramatic affair, almost a coup de théâtre; Berlioz is expressing the satanic spirit, not possessed by it. In Franck's greatest works we feel that the modern rational world is far away, not yet born, that gargoyles are about; that the vaulted roof and half-lights contain the inimical, that soon the bells will resound to expel evil. Franck does not find faith without effort and prayer; and he knows terror. His poetic strength is even naive; and if his technique were not so accomplished, we could call him Bruckner's brother-in-art. But Bruckner was not given the sense of sin; his music is all innocence and patient devotion; moreover, Bruckner takes the scherzo out of the shadows and the terrors and sets it dancing in the genial air and fields of his beloved countryside. The faith won in the D minor Symphony of Franck is won only after a battle. In the opening bar the serpent lifts its head; the phrase is not mine but my master's – Samuel Langford. The wind-instruments supplicate; and towards the end of the first movement the brass sequences, with the main three-note motif, are gigantic in their insistence; the technique of expression here is even related to the desperate brass responses at the climax of the 'Pathétique' Symphony of Tchaikovsky. The allegretto reveals Franck at his beads. The violins intone the credo; then the devils whisper, and again the heavenly host is supplicated; and in the finale, Franck is at his spiritual labours once more, in spite of the carillon echoes that seek an easier solution. Franck is always the penitent; he has neither arrogance nor humour. The style of the romantic grotesque, or the Gothic, has no use for qualities which tell of a purely human mastery. Gothic romance is associated with an elemental naturalism; we feel it in all the major works of Franck. Most of all we feel suggestions of infinitude in his vaulted polyphony, and in the bell-like sonorities which harmonize his music as distance harmonizes the dissonances in nature. Heaven is not always comfortably near at hand for Franck; the cathedral aspires in earnest prayer. He sounds very unlike the father of any French school, ancient or modern.

II

The study of style in music is still in its tentative stages; it really is necessary to take pains to lay stress on Franck's spiritual kinship with medieval romance. The critic of music is at a disadvantage with the critics of literature or of painting or architecture; they can safely refer to, say, Augustan prose, or Metaphysical poetry; or to the styles or schools of Byzantine or Gothic or Barbizon, knowing that most of their readers will understand a generalization under these headings without insisting on a pedantic tightness of definition. It is rare to meet a musician who listens to his art with more than a general sense of tone and style. He feels the broad differences which mark off one composer from another; or one form from another. He understands that each composer has an individual sound, so to say, and his own technical method. But he too seldom understands that the style is not only the man himself but that the man is a product of the Time-Spirit, of the subtly compounded cultural forces of his day and before his day. If the composer is discussed at all, he is subjected to a narrow aesthetic analysis. Or he is tabulated as a link in an evolved chain of technique and style. The forms of music are thought of as though they existed in the abstract, apart from a special act of creation. A scherzo, it is said, is a recognized symphonic form: very well, let us compose one, whether our names be Beethoven, Brahms, Bruckner, Franck or William Walton; whether we belong to the present day or to yesterday, or to a hundred years ago. The truth is that a style or a form of music, as of any other art, depends for convincing life on the psychological make-up of the composer and, even more, on the psychological make-up of his period. A modern adagio is almost as unthinkable as a medieval Rossini crescendo. The difference between a scherzo by Bruckner and one by Beethoven is not a difference of externals, such as the character of the melody, rhythm and harmony employed; it is a difference as great as that which separates pastoral for gnomic poetry. We are obliged to give names to the forms of music, for convenience' sake, just as the forms of architecture have to be named. But a Gothic arch is not a Norman arch. Likewise a Brahms adagio is not a Bruckner adagio. There is an Augustan prose of music;

there is a late school of Barbizon in music; there is certainly a Gothic style in music, even if we have only one great exponent of it, whose name, I maintain, is César Franck. Vincent D'Indy tried to carry Franck's method of medieval symbolism into his musical culture; he lacked his master's power of plastic imagination and particularly his sense of shadows and the demonic.

But the César Franck cathedral is not all belfry and sacristy and cloister; the priest does not renounce the world; he goes forth now and then to proselytize. César Franck persuaded French chamber music – always the woman – to leave the *salon*. By allurements quite sinful in Franck, not by austerity, did he assist conversion. His sonata for piano and violin is amongst the most lyrical composed for the two instruments. True, there is a Fantasia section in which Franck for a moment threatens us with the recitative style used by Beethoven in his address to the Almighty in the Ninth Symphony; Franck begins in D minor, too. We need not quake; the confessional is not directed this time to God (who always has demons in his neighbourhood). Franck is in the private chapel of his cathedral; the suppliant turns poet. There is 'cordial fruit' in the sonata for piano and violin, though of course the music must needs aspire more than once beyond song to prayer. In no other work is Franck more the artist than in the A major Sonata. The cyclic method here does not find him bound to the wheel, like an Ixion of music, as in the symphony we do find him bound, nobly and painfully. The germ-theme is a seed that grows and fructifies without labour; now says the heart of César –

> there is fruit
> And thou hast hands;
> Recover all thy sigh-blown age
> On double pleasures; leave thy cold dispute

Of what is fit and not, forsake thy cage,
Thy rope of sands ...

What an apt phrase is Herbert's 'thy cage' for Franck's
cyclic method! But in the sonata the spirit of his music leaves
the confines; the first movement is a continuous rise and
fall of lyricism, yet warmed with a fullness of harmony
that weds song to meditation. The Recitative-Fantasia is
original in tone and diction, an evocation and a fantasy;
and the flowing canon of the closing allegretto is a rondo of
circling happy, if naively banal, angelicals.

In the string quartet, the burden is taken up again:

O my Saviour make me see
How dearly Thou has paid for me.

The work begins with three descending notes, then a rise
from D to F sharp with another descending phrase; the
music supplicates in upward-reaching fingers; then the
chromatic change at the repetition of the phrase is as a
wringing of the clasped hands. This is an example of
Franck's symbolism; nearly all his music is symbolism;
seldom does he arrange notes for no more than what they
may make *qua* music. Here is an important point to which
I shall return later; to go to Franck for nothing but a
musical satisfaction or experience is as though the Missal
were read for its interest *qua* prose. The D major Quartet is
one of the most massive in existence; the polyphony is
choral in essence and it elevates the chamber style to a
Gothic sublimity of arch. The cyclic method of development
is now once more a penance, a counting of the beads over
and over. Franck toiled at his main theme during its
conception as no composer since Beethoven; but I imagine
that the struggle in Beethoven was as though against lions,
with a fierce joy in it; while César dutifully took up a heavy

cross. In the first movement Franck returns to the task and the search in music which tries to make a synthesis of aspiration and fulfilment – and how shall a saint humbly aspire if fulfilment is granted him? The Lied and sonata elements, so earnestly contrasted in the first movement of the D major Quartet, tell us of César Franck's dualism; of his ceaseless need to importune grace and to receive it like a child. This is the most seraphic of all movements; if ever there was a laying on of hands in music it is when the Lied is heard for the third time and is blessed by the peace of the tonic key.

Then in the Scherzo the devils are at it again. And they come in such artful guise, not honest cohorts of Satan but with whispers of temptation and enchantment. The need is great and César calls on St Ludwig. The Larghetto, in five sections, pronounces the name of the blessed Cavatina; then in the Finale strength is drawn from the bold dialectic of the introduction to the finale of the Ninth Symphony. Franck does not imitate Beethoven; he emulates him, touches his garment to be healed. But he must find his own way. The quartet finishes with Franck on his knees – and at the very last there is the mocking sound of the demons. The spiritual victory is perhaps too easily won; an unguent of chromatic melody, a gleam of light through the stained glass of Sainte-Clotilde; a whiff of incense. Like many saints, Franck's senses were easily titillated; moral austerity in him did not keep him from rather cloying musical delights here and there. There is tinsel in his visions. It is a misuse of language, though, to describe him as a composer capable of theatricality in the slightest. He is absolutely incapable of insincerity; he is never the actor. Of course he accepts the ritual, vestments, incense and all. But if ever a composer wrote out of a humble and contrite heart it was César Franck.

III

The cyclic method of development so prevalent in Franck would have wrecked a composer of less than his force of imagination. By the eternal fitness of things it suited his want of melodic staying-power. There are few melodies of length or variety of phrase in Franck; mostly he composed in small chromatic figures, by sequences now on a higher and now on a lower plane; he extends them in time and space with an 'eternal recurrence' which aptly suits the spiritual basis of his art. The themes float, vanish, return, float away again – it is a sort of winging or hovering of tones and cadences, echoes of the heavenly choir that was never unheard by the inner ear of Franck. The fundamental bell vibrations of his polyphony spread circles of tones and overtones, widening and widening upon the face of his music, expanding to suggestions of infinitude. The same device of overtones apparently comes uncalled to all artists who are trying to express man's aspirations towards the eternal; we can get the sense of this device in the revolving verses at the end of the second part of *Faust*:

> Alles vergängliche
> Ist nur ein Gleichnis ...

but Franck employs a more concrete emphasis than Goethe in *his* revolving peal of heaven's bells. The point to remember is that tones *are* symbols in Franck, and naturally he is constantly symbolizing in the same way the one and only truth. He is much more the priest than the artist; to listen to him in a context of pure artists – with the ear and mind that you give to Mozart, Schubert, or even Beethoven – is as though you were to take down St Augustine from your bookshelf by mistake instead of Molière, Keats or Goethe. The music of Franck is ritual; we must know all the significances. No composer amongst the greatest can be reduced to formulae of expression as small as Franck's. The same chromatic figure or much the same, rising or falling; the same ascents and descents.[1] These motifs are the articles in a credo. They are Canticles, suffused by religious associations which the devout neophyte of Franck soon comes to learn. If we object to the various works of Franck for their sameness or their mannerisms it is as though we should complain that the ritual is always the same, the vestments always the same; the missal and the Blessed Virgin always the same. By the miracle of imagination Franck rings his changes, tells his beads – and lo! they do not remain the same thing the more he changes them. His art is a sort of perpetual transubstantiation of music. Out of three chromatic sounds Franck frames not a fourth sound, but a star. Prelude, Aria and Finale; Prelude, Chorale and Fugue; the Symphonic Variations – God is One and God is Three.

He is not for the market place of the concert halls and the merchants of virtuosi. Leave him in his loft amongst the clouds at Sainte-Clotilde, worshipping God anxiously. Haydn and Bach worshipped with a cheerful heart; Beethoven measured himself with God and stole some of the heavenly fire to light a way to a Promethean truth and eternity. Franck, like Bruckner, was naive at heart, lacking Bruckner's patience because of a more haunted imagination. Bruckner never supplicates; for him God's will be done – in time. There is no hurry in his heart. They are both with God now, Anton and César – this same César, the alleged father of modern French music who was never the sceptic, never the aesthete, never the man of the world or coterie of the

[1] Compare the Lied of the first movement of the quartet with the Recitative of the sonata; compare the main theme of the quintet with the second subject of the finale of the symphony; compare the opening theme of the same movement with the finale of the sonata – here are examples to illustrate my point: the reader will find many more at leisure.

Beaux Arts: César who led the muse of lyricism (pagan, I regret to say) to the baptismal font and made a good Catholic of her.

He belonged to no school of French music, ancient or modern. We incline to forget that Franck trod the same earth as Beethoven; he was born three years before the death of Beethoven. Bruckner was born in 1824, two years after Franck. They are, as I see them, twin souls in art. They will join hands in heaven and compose together; there in bliss they will make music heedless of the busy beat of time, music free at its own gentle will to go on for ever and ever, Amen.

VIII

Debussy
1862-1918

Debussy

THE great sea of Wagner threatened to overwhelm the world of nineteenth-century music until no trace of dry land could be found anywhere. It will never be known how many composers were drowned in the tidal wave; to this day bodies are being washed ashore. A young French musician was caught in the engulfment; but mercifully he struck out and he came to an island. Once he had reached it, he stayed there for ever; an isle of which he might well have said that it was

> ... full of noises,
> Sounds and sweet airs, that give delight and hurt not;
> Sometimes a thousand twangling instruments
> Will hum about mine ears....

High and dry he will dwell in this place of enchantment; he was indeed the Ariel of music, for where should his music be – i' th' air or the earth? Pellucid quiet waters washed his art pure, so that no crude salt from the mightier ocean remained. Though there are usually springs or lakes or fountains and deep murmuring wells in Debussy's music, the sea-change has been magical.

We can understand where most composers come from; with all their originality we can trace their origins. They do not perform acts of spontaneous generation. Bach was the fine fruit from a well-tilled field of polyphony; there is no inexplicable gap of style separating Mozart and Haydn; Beethoven, crossed with Weber, provided the seminal sap

of Wagner; Brahms was a later and fuller flowering of
Schumann; Strauss is an offshoot from Liszt – and Berlioz
was gardener for both of them. The cantilena of Bellini and
the cantilena of Chopin ... All these men needed only their
genius; the soil and the *milieu* waited at hand. Elgar said
that music was in the air to be taken by anybody with ears
keen enough to catch the sound; he meant that music grows
out of itself. There are composers of whom we might say
that if they hadn't hurried and written their music somebody else would have written it for them; it was in the air.
Debussy came from nowhere. In all music extant to 1870
there is not a hint of his advent. Of no other great composer
dare we say that at the time of his birth scarcely a trace is
to be found of the form, the idiom, and the general style
through which his genius in maturity achieved fulfilment
and expression. Mozart, most rare of geniuses, spoke the
language of his period.

Debussy is unique. I hope that nobody will here mention
the whole-tone scale or the name of Mussorgsky. The
whole-tone scale has been overdone in discussions of
Debussy; others besides Debussy have exploited it and have
expressed temperaments and ways of musical conception
different entirely from Debussy's. Mussorgsky certainly
had nothing at all psychologically in common with Debussy,
aristocrat and connoisseur in sensibility. An artist is capable
of assimilating material and responding to suggestions of
technical development without compromising his own
independence of imagination. All genius is a case of internal
combustion; in most cases, though, we can guess where and
from whom they inherited their ignitable stuff; Debussy was
his own storehouse and dynamo of sensibility.

As with the whole-tone scale, much too much has been
made of the influence on him, during his formative years,
of the music he heard at the Exposition Universelle in 1889,

played by the Javanese and Anamite orchestras. The music was almost entirely percussive, and there was little harmony, and much measured beaten-out rhythm. Debussy's music is seldom percussive, nearly always harmonic; and its rhythm is a fluid; a matter of quantity, not of accent. Debussy's interest in the Javanese orchestra and their peculiar tunings, the use of the pentatonic scale and what-not, were phenomena which affected him only externally. The language of a composer, his harmonies, rhythms, melodies, colours and texture, cannot be separated except by pedantic analysis from the mind and sensibility of the artist who happens to be expressing himself through them. The mind and sensibility of Debussy were subtle and indeed unique.

II

We do not come much closer to Debussy's secret by describing him, in his own terms, 'musicien français'. Obviously Debussy's music could not possibly have been written by a German, a Russian, an Englishman, an Italian. For that matter, it could not possibly have been written by any other Frenchman; not by Franck, or by Massenet, or by Fauré, or by Chausson, or by D'Indy, or by Chabrier, to name the French composers who were Debussy's immediate environment at the time that his originality was emerging from the chrysalis. (I cannot seriously consider the view that Ravel's style is at any time indistinguishable from Debussy's; the difference is as great as the difference between a solid and an essence; or between a man of the world and a man aloof.) Debussy evades categories. Say that he is an Impressionist, a painter in music that suggests ethereal vibrations, play of light and shadow, and images of the external universe reflected as though in a mirror of sound. You can support the definition of Debussy as the Monet of his art so long as you keep your ears fixed on certain of the piano works and on the 'Nocturnes'. But where is the Impressionist's absorption in imagery when we come to the Debussy of many of the songs, the 'Chansons de Bilitis', the Villon settings; and, most elusive of all, when we come to *Pelléas*? The opera in itself upsets all the notions of Debussy as an artist who can be fitted into a 'school', a 'tendency', a 'movement'. It is no use changing the label for *Pelléas* and substituting Symbolism for Impressionism. For if you argue to me that in *Pelléas* the music evokes a world of dreams, a world behind the senses, where secret chambers of the Unconscious are opened, where spirits and not men and women are the actors – then I shall flatly deny that Pelléas and Mélisande and Arkel and Golaud are abstractions; they are living and passionate and quiveringly close to us as we watch them and hear them, or overhear them. The forest in which Golaud loses himself is not a metaphysical forest signifying some hidden vault of soul and mind: the orchestra at once tells us, as soon as Golaud intones the words, 'Je ne pourrais plus sortir de cette forêt', that it is indeed a forest in which he is lost, dark and sombre, with long corridors of heavy leafed trees reaching nowhere. When he catches sight of Mélisande sitting by the well, the music tells us exactly what Golaud's eyes have seen. It is all as clear-cut as any musical etching by Richard Strauss. Where is the musical 'symbolism' in Debussy's method of telling us that Mélisande has tossed her ring into the fountain, and that it makes circles on the water as it sinks to the bottom? Richard Strauss does not hang Till Eulenspiegel more unambiguously with his squeak of a wind instrument than Debussy, by a flash of harp, visualizes the ring as it falls, catching the sunlight; then the string harmonies 'plonk' into the depths; for a moment they make a hole in the cool surface of the orchestra, rippling in round and widening circles. I cannot see any difference of *method* in Debussy's musical treatment of this episode and the method employed by Strauss when he sets, in *Don Quixote*, the scene of the rocking horse; the difference is not in method but in the musical sensibility of each composer. Debussy's mind is the more musical; Debussy changed to music every impression his five senses received. In Strauss's psychological make-up there are certain prosaic, or non-musical elements; he is, in a word, not as thoroughly and consistently musical as Debussy. It is not a matter of method but of quality of mind and temperament. Not all things are changed to music that pass through the gateway of the five senses of most composers; Debussy was a reed through which all things blew to music.

Consider again: Mélisande lets her hair fall down from the tower. All the strings in the orchestra fall with it. Actuality is mirrored. But in Debussy, every event in the seen world is subdued to the stuff and state of music; Debussy always translates musically. Strauss and others are content with the appropriate, not necessarily the musical, theme or harmony: Till Eulenspiegel is hung as much with an eye to dramatic effect as with an ear to music.

Debussy was – another paradox – one of the most absolute and pure composers of them all. Whether he was objectively contemplating the poised patterns of nature, or feeling them, or, as Whitman says, 'translating' them; whether he was the absorbed artist in piano vibrations, the first to hear the instrument's overtones; whether he was musician or experimentalist in sonorities; whether he was a poet or dramatist, the end was the same: all things blew through him to music. And how, in the face of *Pelléas* can the legend survive of his aloof Impressionism, Symbolism, or whatever the jargon we use. Mélisande is so pulsatingly alive in her sensibility that I feel that a bad performance of her music would do her almost a physical hurt. She is a Mélisande I know and love; she is not anything as abstract as a symbol. Pelléas is equally alive, impulsive and golden-youthed: his passion sings to the purest lyricism. He is Pelléas, not a symbol. Golaud is a living, lovable, feeling man, with his own texture of nature: he is as much a man as Pelléas is a youth and Mélisande a girl. Arkel is an old man; his music is unmistakably bowed with age and long comprehension of the mystery of life; his music is laden with suffering and wisdom. Compare the characterization of Arkel and of Amfortas. It is Amfortas, not Arkel, who is the symbol, the abstraction, a sort of musical generalization of human pain. Arkel is humanly near us in his every accent. His great cry, 'Si j'étais Dieu, J'aurais pitié de cœur des hommes', is as heart-subduing as anything in the composers we accept as dramatists and humanists.

I shall presently discuss the austere, mystical and dream-like aspects of *Pelléas*, but first I would wish to insist on the fact that the opera is a drama with music, or rather a fairy-story which in its course is seized by a fate and a sorrow beyond its power properly to contain; for it is terrible and almost crude that murder should occur in *Pelléas*, and that the youth of Pelléas should die by the sword.

The characters in *Pelléas* were not mere symbols to Debussy, not abstractions hidden in the vapour of Maeterlinck's mannered mysticism. When he was composing the opera, Debussy wrote of the children of his imagination in this vein: 'I have found myself sadly obliged to finish *Pelléas* while you are so far from me. Moreover, that has not been done without some foot-stamping; the scene between Golaud and Mélisande above all! For it is there that one begins to have a premonition of catastrophes; there, where Mélisande begins to lie and to become enlightened about herself, aided therein by this Golaud, a fine man all the same, who shows that it is not necessary to be entirely frank, even with little girls!'[1]

This is not the language of an artist who is seeing human beings as so many adumbrations of mysticism; a dramatist professedly realistic could scarcely discuss his characters with a more intimate sense of their human relationship. The whole point of *Pelléas*, in fact, as a work of genius for the theatre – and it is of the theatre, and musically has no existence outside the theatre – is that the characters in it are human. It is nature in *Pelléas* that is remote; it is Debussy's treatment of his theme that is withdrawn and mysterious. He does not intrude, or in Wagner's confident way *present*; we should not hear so much as overhear this supremely poignant music-drama, as we sit there, given pre-vision by Debussy until we are as spies of God. The main and characteristic beauty of the work comes from the contrast of frail troubled humans and the eternal impersonal haunts of the night, and whispering lakes and corridors, where silence is a sound and a presence, so that as Debussy himself has written, it is Pelléas and Mélisande who are afraid to speak.

One of Debussy's most acute critics and interpreters, Oscar Thompson, describes him as the poet of mists and fountains, clouds and rains; of dusk and of glints of sun-light through the leaves: 'He was moonstruck and seastruck and a lost soul under a sky besprent with stars.' Debussy was at times all these things. The neglected point is that also he was at times so quiveringly human that compared with him many other composers are pachyderms: prick Mélisande and she will bleed and faint – and the blood will not be stardust mysticism. Is there lack of palpable animal spirits in the 'Villon' ballades? Is there, or is there not, gusto and the flourish of gallantry and the proper robustness in the

[1] Letter to Henri Lerolle in August 1894.

'Song of the Women of Paris'? The energy and comedy of 'Chevaux de Bois' are almost stark and strident; the etching of the music is bold and exhilarating. The style of *La Mer* has even offended the more pallid of the Debussyites, because of the physical exuberance of the brass sonorities; here in Debussy is actually a climax! There is nothing moonstruck about 'Minstrels', 'Hommage à S. Pickwick', 'Mouvement', 'Hommage à Rameau', which last piece has something of the grave firmness which impelled Ingres once to say of a Rameau piece: 'Marble!' In Debussy's 'Hommage' we can see the veins in the marble, but the strength is implicit always.

I do not wish to labour the point and exaggerate to prove a case; Debussy's temperament and style were not of the world that is commonly called normal. He was not a full man; he was intense. But he was not narrow and inhumane. To read the average estimate of Debussy, one would imagine that he was only a chapter in the history of the development and subtilization of French sensibility; and in music mainly a necromancer in the chemistry of tone, a dweller in the Ivory Tower of the late nineteenth-century aestheticism. No wonder that towards the end of his life he wished to achieve something different – 'an effect of reality'. The French of that now sadly receding day could scarcely ever discover a genius without dragging him into a movement.

III

In this book I shall bring in here and there one or two themes or leading-motives and try to develop them into the general texture with some symphonic aptness and enlargment. One of these themes is that a composer is always likely to suffer misunderstanding more than most artists by reason of the nature of his material; music is a thing in

itself, a language *sui generis*: few people are born with what
Jules Combarieu called the 'pensée musicale'.[1] I have
known in a life devoted to music only a few minds capable
of thinking and feeling musically. It is easy then to realize
how a composer who, like Debussy, cannot be at once related
to a common background of idiom and style is bound to be
misunderstood for years. The trouble is that first and false
estimates of such a composer crystallize into accepted truth;
and the legend is hard to knock on the head.

If I were asked to define Debussy in a few words (an
unreasonable but irresistible challenge) I should first say
that he is a composer of abnormal intellectual subtlety, for
I count sensibility as much a matter of vibrations of mind
as of the senses. Then I should add that because of this
intellectual subtlety he is acutely aware of the overtones of
existence, human and of nature, and that he expressed his
consciousness and experience as artist in music so precise and
fastidious that it is without obscurity or irrelevance.

The general view of Debussy – I need hardly say – is
exactly contrary. He is regarded as an artist in musical
ambiguities, all sensory reactions to colour and atmosphere;
no outlines but many changing iridescent hues; a dreaming
faun of the 'nineties, more of an aesthete than anything else,
evoking half-tones and elliptical silences and – as the man
in Tchekov says – all the rest of it. The truth is that in no
composer since Mozart has the single note, or group of
notes, meant so much as in Debussy. A score by him is as
interdependent and as economical in its constituent parts
as a perfect mathematical formula. Or to use a tenderer
simile, each note in Debussy is a star in a firmament where

[1] Jules Combarieu: 'Les rapports de la musique et de la poésie, considerées au
point de vue l'expression': 'The musician thinks with sounds as the littérateur
thinks with words. It is a mysterious privilege but indubitable. Not only do
poet and musician not speak the same language nor obey the same laws but
they do not think with the same faculty.'

the law of musical poise and taste is supreme and where not a sparrow of a demi-semiquaver ever falls without reason.

Debussy is reticent, not restricted, in expression. The world he created is not small or sicklied over with a mannered aestheticism. We have seen that in *Pelléas* there is a poignant enough echo of the sad human threnody; we have agreed, too, that in the songs there are life and variety. Also there is *La Mer*, vibrant with dawn and the sound of the sea, music which is a world of ocean not an impression of it; all the mythology of the sea is here given delighted life; dolphins and waves are at play under vast stretches of sky full of billowing winds. And in all the rainbow tumult, orchestration of sun and spray, we hear the triton's horn – this is the happiest music I know, the most enchanted.

He created a new music at the end of the nineteenth century; he led the way from the cul-de-sac of Wagner; he dissolved the solids and primary colours of the keyboard; he purified French song by wedding it again to the natural rise and fall of the French language. He disdained fashions; he was the most independent-minded of artists. He had the surest ear and the finest musical aesthetic of all the composers of his day. He was refined and judicious to the last demi-semiquaver. This is the composer who has been grouped with the French decadents and labelled *fin de siècle*, presumably because he first came to prominence by an orchestral work (of classic coolness and precision!) based on a poem by Mallarmé.

IV

The fastidious aesthetic of Debussy deceived his contemporaries into thinking that his music was short of inner power, rhythm, passion. To be dramatic in Debussy's day meant that a composer was under an obligation to exploit the orchestral crescendo, and beat up excitement by mounting sequences. There are no peaks by orchestral climax in *Pelléas*; no whippings up of the nerves by repetition and acceleration. Hence we have been told that *Pelléas* is not dramatic, except in a vague way that can be felt only if we react to the music in some tenuous and complicated state of our souls. If there is no palpable drama in the fact that Golaud, human and visible, is lost in Debussy's dim murmuring forest, then I do not know what drama is; we feel that he is being enveloped by strange forces that are about to change his destiny — his destiny here and now on earth, not in a metaphysical unknown or void. If there is no drama, palpable and of the theatre, when Debussy's music sends the frightened doves fluttering from the tower, I am at a loss to account for the pulsations of my imagination at this point of the score. I know few moments in opera more definitely dramatic than when Pelléas, at the approach of Golaud, ejaculates, 'Attends! attends!' and the orchestra palpitates in triplets — timpani triplets at that! — and pizzicato. The crisis is all over within the space of a dozen bars; but its brevity only leaves the scene more sharply etched. When Mélisande's hair tumbles from the tower over the face of Pelléas, all the violins — as I have said — fall down with it in golden tresses of tone, technically called chords of the seventh; is this not open and palpable drama and, like the music which tells us of the flash of Mélisande's ring into the fountain, is it not graphically dramatic, and in need of no equivocating allusions to 'Symbolism'?

In Debussy's period to be lyrical meant that a composer was obliged to vaunt his melody, all arching to an apex of high notes, with an appoggiatura — if time there should be for one — to squeeze out the last juices. Well, there is even lyricism of this recognizable order refined to the purest essence in the ecstatic 'Je les joue' of Pelléas. But lyricism is a mode of feeling, not just a style of opera composition; all that happens in *Pelléas*, vocally and orchestrally, is infused with the feeling and therefore the style of lyric-drama. It is an odd thought – *Pelléas*, one of the few operas where recitative and melody are equally warmed by music, and it is impossible to say where the one ends and the other begins, this is the opera which has frequently been praised for everything except its sustained lyrical style. Any music not lyrical, say a stretch of recitative from an opera by Massenet, supposedly the master of lyric-drama at its most suave, would have coarsened the tissue of *Pelléas* like a strand of sackcloth through silk.

In Debussy's period, rhythm meant emphasis, a succession of balanced bar-phrases. We need not at this time of day interrupt our argument to point out the presence in Debussy's music of rhythm; the development of music since the late 'nineties has concentrated much on the subtilization of rhythm and the liberating of melody and harmony from the tight-pinching boots of pointed emphasis. I cannot imagine that any musician of today will quote the old rigid definitions of rhythm to prove that Debussy was weak in rhythm. Yet without implying that Debussy's pulse is even weak, we can agree that because of Debussy's preoccupation with harmonic problems the movement of his music tended to proceed in flowing lengths not sharply or abruptly changed; Wagner, when he was similarly preoccupied with the harmonic discoveries and revelations in *Lohengrin*, composed nearly the whole work in four-four time. It is difficult for a composer to be simultaneously flexible of rhythm and rich and subtle in harmonic mutation. Rhythm in Debussy is less a melodic than harmonic constituent. I often feel that not until he had composed a stretch of music was it possible for him to write the time-signatures of the different divisions; in a word, I feel he had to wait until after he had brought his music into life before he could apply his fingers to it to count the pulse. A Debussy rhythm is a heartbeat, not a tick-tick of a metronome.

So with form in Debussy; his period regarded form in music more or less as sonata-form: a preliminary statement, a development with licence to indulge in a free fantasia, then a recapitulation. I am not amongst those students of musical physiology who are prepared to dismiss sonata-form in its widest and subtlest manifestations as a mechanical device necessary only to a certain state in the history and evolution of the art. I am not at all sure that sonata-form with fugal form do not comprise the two main categories in the musical consciousness; or, to use less technical language, they are perhaps the only two possible ways in which we can think intelligibly in music. Growth seems, in all things, to combine fugal and sonata-form; a beginning, an unfolding, an expanding movement of organic fibre; a blossoming, then a cadential and dying fall to a point of rest that recalls the beginning, as the last leaf of the tree seeks again the earth. The arch of a bridge is sonata-form; and in sentimental language we may say that ashes to ashes, the course of life, is also sonata-form. I do not see how the art of music, which more than any other art is dependent on its own design to be intelligible at all, can ever throw sonata-form entirely aside, though of course I do not mean by this that the old rigid compartments must not be more and more subtilized and rendered flexible and interchangeable. The other arts can erect themselves on scaffolding drawn from tangible life itself: the shape of a play follows the logic of human nature and events; a painting has its objectively perceived design. Music must make its own design and logic as it goes along: the difficulty is that music-form is not an object in space, but an object in time only.

It is easy, then, to say that Debussy threw the old forms

aside. (He did not throw them entirely aside, as I shall presently show.) He rejected the straitjacket of development – as Oscar Thompson says: he avoided repetition for repetition's sake. But what is form in Debussy; how does he put his music together; what is the architectural logic? It is no use replying to this question with airy generalizations about Debussy's creative imagination instinctively finding its own form. This language deals with the hidden processes of conception; I wish to discover the ground-plan of a Debussy composition as it stands *now* – after it has been conceived and given in black and white to the world. How does it achieve anatomy and organic life, emerge note by note to a balanced whole, with beginning and end inevitably related? I confess I have not read a single illuminating analysis of Debussy's form; all we have been told is that he freed music from the old shackles and created a form of his own. What is this form, what is the rationale? Form in Debussy is not amorphous, as the early critics thought it was, when they could not find it in the old fingerposts of sonata-form.

In the smaller pieces, the problem is not difficult. On a more or less miniature surface you can achieve self-sufficiency of pattern by comparatively few colours or few lines. The changeful floating play of harmonies in, say, 'Reflets dans l'Eau', make a balanced sequence, and express moods that end as soon as expressed – lovely, fleeting shadows and sungleams. (Yet even in 'Reflets dans l'Eau' the tracings of an A-B-A ground-plan are discernible.) It is in the shaping of a five-act lyric-drama that a more comprehensive method of design is needed than any I have so far had revealed to me in his music by students and critics who have studied design in Debussy and published their discoveries. Mr Oscar Thompson tells us that Debussy's music does not develop in the traditional sense, but that

each melodic fragment, each chord, has its own expressive-
ness in the unified succession of sonorities. 'There is little
building from measure to measure.' This is like saying that
in the form of a tree there is no branching from branch to
branch, but that the tree achieves its own expressive tree-
ness in the unified succession of its sap and leaves. Music
is obliged to be composed from measure to measure;
Pelléas certainly does not hang together by virtue of
separate parts; it is not a pastiche. Debussy himself said: 'I
should like to see the creation – I myself shall achieve it –
of a kind of music free from themes and motives, or formed
on a single continuous theme, which nothing interrupts,
and which never returns upon itself.' Did he achieve his
ideal? It is to *Pelléas* that we must turn for an answer; for, as
I say, the larger the surface to cover, the severer the test of a
composer's power to write organically developed music.

Debussy did not ever write a kind of music free from
themes and motives, and formed on a single continuous
theme which never returns upon itself. In his smallest pieces
there is usually a recapitulation somewhere, either of theme
or group of themes. The creative artist fortunately over-
looks his theories; it would have been as impossible to
create a long opera from one theme as a play from one character. In *Pelléas*, Debussy went so far as to swallow a dish of
prejudice and employ a set of representative themes. 'I hate
the leit-motif', he said once on a time, 'not only when it is
abused, but even when it is used with taste and discernment.'
Debussy used leading-motives in *Pelléas* with the utmost
taste and discernment: the Mélisande theme – to name only
one example – returns many times during the course of
the opera. But Debussy's themes are not self-consciously
representative. They do their identifying work indirectly;
they do not seem aware of their function. They do not, so
to say, pry or point with the finger. They are fugitive and

discreet. A voice is echoed, a movement or a gesture is seen at a glance, a ripple of wind disturbs a pool of silent thought; there is a cry in the night – the Debussy leading-motive is evocative, not representative. The Wagner orchestra, like Strauss's, is a commentator; Debussy's orchestra, in *Pelléas*, is a quiet mirror which catches images from a world unconscious that it is casting reflections at all. None the less, Debussy uses themes and repetitions in his own way – as other composers have used similar devices in their own ways – to make the stuff of his instrumental tissue, to give it shape. Instinct led him, in spite of his theory, towards proven methods of achieving a unity in which the parts would own allegiance to a whole. What's to come is not unsure in the making of music – or should not be.

If we examine the structure and sequence of the music of *Pelléas* in one or two main centres, we shall find that Debussy honoured, as Wagner and most composers have honoured, a logic based on the ritornello, a return to a starting point, or an echo of it, an arching process in which the end is perceived in the beginning. After Golaud says, 'Je suis perdu aussi', at the end of the first scene, there is a distinct return to the beginning of the same scene, not of course a crude note-for-note return, but a return to, or recollection of, texture and mood. Again, in the scene by the fountain in the park: the episode ends with Pelléas saying: 'La verité; la verité'; the music, in theme and instrumental colour, echoes the beginning of the scene, nor merely by use of a motif; it is a renewal of texture, a psychological harking-back for design's sake, an internal as well as an external rounding-off. The unifying of the tissue of *Pelléas* is not always as easy as this to reduce to a pattern at once demonstrable without aid of musical quotations so numerous that whole pages of the score would have to be reproduced. Sometimes Debussy balances a theme or a harmonic group

or an instrumental colour; sometimes these factors are interchanged; sometimes the pattern is less one of theme,
harmony, rhythm, than of atmosphere and mood, imperceptibly contrasted. But throughout the different tableaux
there is some such comprehensive organization, in which
measure is related to measure. Like the Catastrophe in the
old comedies, sonata-form will jump into all music, at the
cue, in cunning disguises. It is only when Debussy attends
to his theory of no motifs, no interruptions and returnings
of music on itself – only then does the score of *Pelléas* seem
to meander; only then does Debussy merely underline
Maeterlinck's text without making, as Ernest Newman has
pointed out, the musical tissue really organic.[1]

The irony (or joke, if you like) about Debussy and
Pelléas is that Debussy, after violently reacting against the
Wagner theory of music-drama, conformed much more
rigidly to it than Wagner himself. Debussy, far more than
Wagner, obeyed the Wagerian fiat that drama must be the
end aimed at in opera, and music only the means. Wagner
became too vastly consumed by music, when he got down
to the job and the heart of the matter, to place himself at
the beck and call of the dramatist, even though the dramatist was Richard Wagner and no other. In all his masterpieces he let his own theory of music-drama go hang, and
gave us operas which are the greatest, at least the most
opulent, glorification of music ever experienced in the
theatre, with 'endless melody', and symphonic development. From a narrowly musical point of view, *Pelléas* could
justifiably be described as a denial of song and music alike;
Debussy asks for self-abnegation in his vocalists, who for the
most part have to content themselves with semi-chant, or
parlante, a kind of recitative adumbrating a series of musical
phrases yet remaining part of the French language in tone

[1] *A Music Critic's Holiday*, p. 200.

and accentuation. This speech-song is wonderfully woven into the orchestral tissue, there are no separable vocal patterns, no (if I may set teeth on edge by using the term in this context) 'numbers'.

There is another ironic connection which *Pelléas* has with the aesthetics of music-drama. Debussy here makes music a means in the scheme of opera and drama the end; he puts the musical genius at the service of Maeterlinck. The piquancy comes in when it is realized that Maeterlinck's drama is all the time aspiring to the condition of music. Maeterlinck uses words to evoke music, or moods which music can feed on; his drama reaches out towards those fluid impersonal sorts of feeling which, as Wagner would say, contain 'the stuff of music'. But Debussy often holds back the powers of music, in *Pelléas*, to the extent of depriving his singers of fully licensed melody. Recitative at its most eloquent or suggestive is only a kind of prose of music. It is because some of us receive a hint – and more than a hint – of aesthetic cross-purposes in *Pelléas* that we cannot get quite through a performance without uneasy moments of a sense of tedium. None the less, I would go far and give much to sit once again, from beginning to end, through *Pelléas and Mélisande*, one of the longest of all operas – which is another ironic stroke indeed; for Debussy was usually sarcastically against the large-scaled, thoroughly worked-out species of composition. *Pelléas* is a music-drama of genius all the same. And the core of the work's genius, for the analyst of technique, is in the disposition of harmony and the orchestration. After all, it was the right instinct that impelled Debussy to the chant-speech vocal style of *Pelléas*. French opera, because of influences too 'grand', an impact of Meyerbeer and Wagner, had evolved a vocal swagger or swell of line unsuitable to the true sources of French song and singing. These alien influences forced even

Saint-Saëns to a bastard impurity of style. The vocal arch and rhetoric even of parts of *Carmen* are imported and do damage to accent and nuance of the French language. A Chanson is not a Lied or an Aria, and never can be cultivated to grow into one. The 'Chansons de Bilitis' are at the extreme to song as immediately understood by German, French, Italian or English ears. So Debussy might have answered our indictment – that *Pelléas* is a denial of song – by saying: 'Yes; of all song not born out of French words, accents and the essential tones, and accents of the French voice.' Let us leave it at that.

V

It is a mistake to imagine that when Debussy turned to traditional forms at the end of his life he achieved a complete *volte face* in his technique of organization. The three sonatas written between 1915 and 1917 are comparatively low-pulsed and failing in inspiration not because Debussy suddenly reacted from so-called Impressionism to neo-Classicism, but simply because he was a dying man. The String Quartet, surely a Debussy work if ever there was one, in style as well as in its sensibility, draws upon many a device of classical form. Debussyites of the nebulous school actually objected to signs in 'La Mer' of thematic connection and synthesis, and 'La Mer' was composed between 1903-5. There is no evidence that Debussy did not always mingle aristocratic reserve, subtlety of sensibility with the most refined appreciation of the logic of form developed and honoured through the ages.

At bottom, though, the art of this most fastidious of composers, who never wrote an ugly descriptive passage, needed impulse and fertilization from the visible world; from sights and sounds; from light and movement; from the changing colours of morning, noon and night; from the harmonies of dawn and sunset; from nature physical and also from nature human – from the moods of the sensitive ones that inhabit the earth. He needed, too, some echo from the world that is invisible and conjecturable. Given these quickenings, his imagination turned everything to music pure and undefiled.

IX

Edward Elgar
1857-1934

Edward Elgar

E LGAR was one of the last of the composers of our time to keep in touch with the musical public at large – he and Strauss. Today the composer chooses to remove himself from the mass of reasonably intelligent listeners; he deliberately cultivates a strange language; he is determined not to sound like any other composer; he has a contempt for the familiar style; he would perish rather than write music easy to understand and remember. On principle he impels his hair to rise on end at the mere mention of romanticism. One of the chief objections directed against Elgar by the more strenuously contemporary musicians is that he frequently lapses into the commonplace and was not fastidious enough. Elgar was actually unashamed of his 'Pomp and Circumstance' marches; and the fact that he was not ashamed of them is regarded by his detractors as an added enormity; they could no doubt forgive vulgarity in Elgar had he exploited it cynically. But no, he was frankly proud of 'Land of Hope and Glory'; he once declared with some heat (and no little accuracy) that it was 'a damned fine popular tune'.

To aggravate matters he did not look like an artist and a composer, but more like an English gentleman. Worse still, he wrote a lot of music which obviously is the music of an English gentleman. So what with his 'vulgarity' and his 'respectability', how possibly could he be classified and reduced to a system or a movement? In a period which like the present regards the creative faculty as self-conscious and rationally directed, Elgar's indifference to an organized aesthetic has aroused the gravest misgivings. He founded and encouraged no school; he was capable of composing a military march one day and music for an oratorio the next. In a lecture delivered from the chair of an English university, Elgar on an occasion stated that most contemporary composers were at heart formalists who addressed themselves too much to their own craft; they were afraid of vulgarity, which, he maintained, 'would have been preferable, for vulgarity might have shown signs of initiative'. He was a direct man and as direct in his music. 'I put the whole of myself into it,' he declared, 'I keep nothing back.' He was wise; the greatest composers sound as they look; I am convinced of this theory. A turn of phrase, a harmonic flavour, a colour of instrumentation, is as revealing as the sound of a voice or a gesture or a movement, as a man talks or walks. Wagner's music could not have come from the heart and mind of a reticent individual; I see the face of Beethoven in all that he composed. The paradox is that music, the most intensely emotional of the arts, can express not only passionate and full-blooded men but men of reticence; music can burn with Wagner's flame of rhetoric and can freeze with the few rational words of Sibelius. Look at a photograph of Sibelius – it is just like his music, even to the baldness.

Elgar and his music are one and indivisible. The man who wrote *Gerontius* was the man who wrote the broad and healthy Introduction and Allegro for Strings. It was the one and the same Elgar who wrote *Falstaff* and the 'Nursery' Suite. He was a full and human being. And to those who knew him he was great, not only in his largest and loftiest conceptions but in his simple English failings.

II

Elgar liked to know that ordinary folk enjoyed his music. 'I give them all that is in me.' He well knew that if genius in a full man is tampered with, or drawn on meticulously, if you pick and choose from the largesse given by the gods to you, then you may well miss something good, or stifle at birth an inspiration. You must accept trustfully the full cornucopia of the muses and not look the gift in the mouth. Gusto is the first sign of genius, which nobody can deny, not even the contemporary fashion in good manners, the fashion which prefers the small man and perfect artist to the big man and not so perfect artist. Basil Maine tells how Elgar entertained some friends one night to a gramophone concert in his country house. He put on records of his own *Falstaff* and during the first interlude – the Dream Picture – he listened absorbedly, then said: 'That is what I call *music.*' I doubt if he made a distinction between his own music in particular and music and the spirit of music in general. It was his opinion that music is in the air – 'music is all around us; the world is full of it, and you simply take as much of it as you require'. In brief, Elgar believed in inspiration; he did not compose according to a preconceived aesthetic or 'system'; he was self-taught and reached middle-age before he wrote a mature individual work. Then, in a sudden spate, over a period of only fifteen years, he produced his masterpieces: the 'Enigma' Variations, *Gerontius*, the two symphonies, the Introduction and Allegro for Strings, the Violin Concerto, and *Falstaff*. He could not compose at all until he grew as a man – then where, you may well ask, is the notion that he believed in inspiration? Inspiration, you are at liberty to point out, does not wait on time and birthdays and experience. Is it not suspicious, you may ask, that Elgar produced no work of consequence until he had learned the elaborate orchestral technique of his day: in other words, the tricks of his trade? The plain truth is that he *was* obliged to learn his language. Inspiration does not woo the artist who is not a master of technique waiting in a field rich of soil for a sowing. Music may be 'in the air', but in the England of Elgar's youth quick ears were needed to catch it and make it one's own. I can think of no greater composer who took his rise from an environment as unpromising to his art as Elgar's when he was a young man. England in those years was solemnly and surely 'Das Land ohne Musik'. Elgar lived for long in his formative years in the narrowest of holes and corners of culture – Worcester and the West Country – not amongst the yokels thereof but in the presence, day by day, of the dull middle-classes. A sojourn in London relieved the comfortable monotony – a London the art and music of which had about as much to do with the life and history and the crises of man's imagination as any exhibition at the Royal Academy of the canvases of Leighton, Landseer, Sidney Cooper. Oscar Wilde assured the world that Frith's 'Derby Day' was 'all done by hand'; it can be stated with equal veracity that when Elgar was changing from youth to manhood nearly all English music was composed 'by ear' by men conscientiously educated in the more acceptable of the German classics. I can discover no evidence that in the London of the 'eighties music or painting or the theatre were regarded as necessary to the fulfilment and clarifying of mankind's experience as temporal or immortal beings. Bach was a subject of academic study; and Wagner was a season at Covent Garden. When, in 1908, the A flat Symphony of Elgar was played for the first time, those of us who were students were excited to hear at last an English composer addressing us in a spacious way, speaking a language which was European and not provincial. No English symphony existed then, at least not big enough to make a show of comparison with a symphony by Beethoven or Brahms and go in the programme of a concert side by side with the acknowledged masterpieces, and not be dwarfed at once into insignificance. I was present at the Hallé Concert on December 3rd, 1908, when Hans Richter conducted the first performance of the A flat Symphony; I can see his huge bulk to this day, as he stood, back to the eager audience; he lifted his arms slightly and obtained silence; then the broad tune, with the grave steady tread of the double-basses underneath, came upon our ears. What a long first subject, we said – how original! Then the sudden double-bar pause, then the plunge into a remote key and a forging energy; fountains of string tone, brass instruments in ricochet; no such virtuoso orchestration had been heard by us before in the music of an Englishman, or of any other composer; for Strauss was not familiar to us in that distant backward and abysm of time. The Elgar string divisions opened our enchanted ears upon new faery seas of tone; the muted brass of the closing cadences of the adagio was revealed magic. Elgar put English music on the map of Europe; we could play a work by him in any programme of symphonic dimensions and pretensions. I cannot hope, at this time of day, to describe the pride taken in Elgar by young English students of that far-away epoch. The irony is that young English musicians who affect to despise Elgar nowadays be-cause of his 'reactionary tendencies' do so from a point of vantage won for them by Elgar himself.

It is amusing, the tendency at the present time towards nationalism in music once more; Elgar is looked at suspici-ously because he employed the technique of the nineteenth-century symphonists of Europe. In *our* young days we were grateful to Elgar for sweeping English music into the main stream, out of the local backwater. Elgar is now attacked on the one hand for his Edwardian mentality; in the next breath he is charged with eclecticism. He is said to write affably and complacently in the manner of (*a*) Brahms, (*b*) Schumann, (*c*) Strauss and (*d*) César Franck; because presumably he took the symphonic and orchestral technique as he found it. It is the mark of casual criticism not to note differences in things superficially alike. Bruckner is accused of Wagnerisms because, poor naive soul, he blew down the tenor and bass tubas employed by Wagner in the 'Ring'.

Elgar was as individual as any other composer. I do not mean that he wrote original music all the time; often he repeated in his own way the substance of other and greater composers; or rather he followed paths trodden by them but spoke his own thoughts as he did so. It would be possible to identify the authorship of a single bar of Elgar's music written on a torn scrap of manuscript found in a dustbin. The critic who cannot see through the assimilated stuff in Elgar to the man himself, and is unable to distinguish between acquired and inherited characteristics, merely demonstrates his incapacity to listen intelligently to music at all. Whether one 'likes' or 'dislikes' Elgar's music is a personal issue, beside the critical question. Elgar's music is not anonymous and not synthetic; it is his own, and because he was a representative man of his period it sums up a great epoch in English life and history. There is a cant in contemporary criticism to the effect that a man's music is valuable only in so far as it has influence on the technique and form of music of the future. We must be progressive at all costs; we must constantly achieve a 'new synthesis'. Whether a composition is characteristic in itself, without aim or hope of shaping the destiny of music at large, is a point seldom taken into account. All of which is the talk of the dilettante, mostly young. I doubt if any great artist has opened new paths, or has thought of opening them. The tiller of the field is not the reaper of the harvest. History of music shows that few works of lasting quality have come from the experimentalists in technique and form. Philipp Emanuel Bach was the 'progressive'; today we have forgotten him and remember the conservative Johann Sebastian, who took the language and media of music as he found it. If Elgar is not a great composer the proof will not be demonstrated by pointing to the devices he borrowed from the symphonic and instrumental technique accumulated during the nineteenth century. Did he employ the cyclic method of development in his A flat Symphony? ... Very well then, so he did. 'Das sieht jeder Narr!' Did Shakespeare 'originate' the sonnet form?

Elgar is no more imitative than a tree is imitative of another tree that happens to grow from the same soil. What need was there for Elgar to work out a new form? He was in at a rich garnering. Geniuses are wise to study the calendar, and time their coming by the harvest moon. Elgar wrote the last of the epic symphonies; Sibelius saw the last sheaves bound and carried away and he sought for fresh pastures, in his Seventh Symphony, which is formally of worth but musically inferior to his Second and Fifth. The symphony as an expression of the tragical-ethical, tragic-comical, historical and rhetorical, came to an end with Brucker, Brahms, Mahler, César Franck and Elgar. The busy world decided to leave Elgar more or less to the English as soon as the fact was established that his cosmopolitanism was superficial, only a matter of form and technique naturally adapted to an English outlook and temperament – moreover an Edwardian outlook. I do not think a composer is to be valued less if he happens to communicate a national or regional secret. Such a composer may not rank with the highest and universal geniuses. But there is a greatness of blood and race and of period as well as the greatness of widespread view that surveys mankind from China to Peru.

We who have listened to Elgar during the music festivals held in the cathedral cities of Worcester, Gloucester and Hereford at the time of ripening summer know his secret. Here at the harvest of the year, in country washed by the rivers of the west, we have known music as music everywhere should be; part of the soil, creative, free, serious, life-giving. The thought that an art has grown up from the very ground you are treading and is bearing its fruits all around you is something very different from the feeling that it has been brought to you from a long way. Elgar in his own countryside was, like Bruckner at Linz, more than a maker of music for concerts; he was an informing spirit, of the air and the environment that made us alive. One mellowing afternoon in September I listened to the A flat Symphony in the cathedral at Worcester. Where I was seated, at my side, lay a sculptured knight, arms folded. The light of the living day came through the stained-glass windows; the past and the present mingled in the eternity of the arched roof. I think it was Schlegel who said that architecture is frozen music. On this afternoon it was as though the old stone and the windows and tracery became audible in Elgar's music. And through the symphony's graver strains we heard also the exhilaration of brass bands, sturdy marching rhythms, and sunset cadences; this was a symphony in which an Englishman praised God and praised his country. I am neither patriotic in a political sense nor religious. The same could have been said of Bernard Shaw. Yet on this occasion in Worcester Cathedral both Shaw and myself sat and listened to the A flat Symphony and were moved to our foundations. Let Kipling's devil ask as much as he likes: 'But was it art?'

Here we are at the truth about Elgar. He was the

destined laureate of the burgeoning age of Edward VII. Though he was born in 1857 he would have left no important mark on music had he died at the age of forty in the year of Queen Victoria's Diamond Jubilee. Under Edward VII the inhibitions of Victorianism had given way to some spaciousness; opulence came forth honestly in fine feathers. The Empire and the spirit thereof were as a pageant now, not a chapter in the history of buying in the cheapest market and selling in the dearest. For nine years it was high noon over the seven seas; not a cloud was to be seen on the clear sky of Britain's splendour. Elgar's music emerged from the period as the plant from the fruitful soil. His works are abstracts and by no means brief chronicles of the times. Here is the music of peace and plenty. Pomp and circumstance and Buckingham Palace and the Mall and Westminster, all poised in a crescendo and cadence of fulfilment – *nobilimente*. The flag is unfurled, waving possession not belligerence; the trumpet and drum of satisfied conquest are alternated with the cathedral's thanksgiving for all the good things vouchsafed to His chosen people by the Lord. The terrace and the country house and the major-general and the gaitered bishop and the group of noble dames.... So the pageant of Elgar's music passes: Oxford movement and Church militant, the trooping of the colour and evensong, children in Kensington Gardens and Phil May's cockneys; the ripening pippin in Gloucestershire, and the tumult of the Spithead review.

This is the conventional view of Elgar, and some of his critics see no deeper. What of the other Elgar who plays hide-and-seek behind the panoply of ceremonial orchestration and massed choralism; what of the poet who for long is concealed under the robes of the official singer of tribal lays? There was a major-general actually in the Elgar family, on his wife's side; and his music is constantly emitting the explosions of the parade ground. But there is the dreamer in the cloisters, the man with the musing eye, the Englishman when he is alone. We look at Elgar's portrait and admire the patrician nose, the military moustaches; we think superficially that the eye sees what the ear hears from much of his music; then we are reminded of the macabre beginning of *Gerontius* and we are reminded, too, of the fresh early-morning air of the aubade of the Serenade for Strings. *Falstaff* looms large as life as he walks like a sow overwhelming her litter before other creatures of Elgar's fancy, such as the 'Dorabella' variation, fine-spun gossamer of sound; the swirling Arielesque scherzo of the Second Symphony; the cradle-song of the slow movement of the String Quartet; the hushed peacefulness of the beginning of the second part of *Gerontius*.

Elgar was many-sided, after the nature of a genius and great man. Is he complacent in the closing section of the Second Symphony? Not more so than he is bodeful in the largo of the same work; here is a profounder 'Recessional' than Kipling's. He is English to an extent that all critics not English are baffled by contradictions of psychology and character of the kind that bewildered Taine. Man of action and private poet and Empire laureate, he is tangible and elusive; he is country squire and major-general and the devotee at prayer. He is austere and vulgar and prosaic and romantic; he is the Catholic whose oratorios are acceptable to the most venerable adherents of the Anglican Church; in short he is English. And in nothing was Elgar more English and of his period than in his shrewd adaptation of the best continental models; Free Trade in composition. When Richard Strauss and Hans Richter hailed *Gerontius* and the A flat Symphony as masterpieces and welcomed them into the commonwealth of Europe's music, these men probably understood the external shape, the parts of speech, before they heard the essential Englishness. There is a surface allegiance to *Parsifal* expressed in the prelude of *Gerontius*. The A flat Symphony honours the continental symphonic procedure, from the adagio of the Ninth Symphony of Beethoven to the cyclic method of development of César Franck. None the less, under the skin of everything flows the blood of an Englishman.

III

In hell there is, I hope, a special circle of fire and ice for the people who cannot listen to music without hunting down the resemblances, identities, or as they call them with little regard for good English, reminiscences. They hunt them down with all the enthusiasm of short-sighted detectives. They are like wine-tasters, more concerned about authenticity than enjoyment. They confuse novelty of sound with originality of idea; they would have regarded Homer as entirely derivative.

'Listen,' they say, as they attend to Elgar's *In the South*; 'Strauss's divided strings; *Aus Italien* all over again.' Or when it is a performance of *The Music-Makers*: 'Hark! Strauss again; he quotes himself ... *Heldenleben*, flat burglary as ever was!' The 'cello phrases at the end of *Falstaff* inevitably draw these solvers of musical crosswords: '*Don Quixote!*' is the unanimous chorus. Elgar no doubt emulated the orchestration of Strauss during one phase of his development; he seemed almost to translate him for the delectation of English ears. The opening section of *The Dream of Gerontius* inhabits the still dread chamber of the beginning of *Tod und Verklärung*. But from a more or less similar point of departure the lines of Strauss and Elgar diverge spiritually to contrary poles. Elgar was a more earnest craftsman and his purpose was loftier. He could never have descended to the level of Strauss in *Josephlegende*; an Elgar military march may be vulgar; never insincere. It is the absence of cynicism in Elgar that disturbs the sophisticated young ear of these days. To the sleuths who seek assiduously to pluck disguises from the face and body of Elgar's music I herewith make the present of another clue. The Brahms–Strauss fingerprints are misleading. Let the investigation be carried in the direction of Bruckner; there is a likeness between the two composers in their main styles and attitudes to music, allowing for the difference between two brands of Catholicism, and also allowing for the difference between Styria and the Malvern Hills. Bruckner was not interested in any empire of this earth, and Elgar made the most of two worlds. Bruckner was sometimes naive to the point of ineffectuality as a technician; and Elgar was master of the orchestra. Yet the spiritual connection of Elgar with Bruckner is most marked; he sounds the deep religious adagio note of Bruckner in his slow movements; he praises the open air, like Bruckner. Bruckner, though, is the peasant and child of God; Elgar is of the English middle-classes and a Churchman. And both are esteemed in their own countries and not abroad.

Elgar's erudition and craftsmanship could not hide a nature which was as lovable at bottom and as simple as Bruckner's. Consider how he prepared himself to write a symphonic-poem on the subject of Falstaff. He discovered a fact not known to all English folk, the fact that the Falstaff of *The Merry Wives of Windsor* is not the real Falstaff. He then read all the Shakespearean commentaries he could lay his hands on and would no doubt have gone as far in his studies as a scrutiny of the treatise of the learned gentleman in Dickens, the scholar who discovered that by altering the punctuation of Shakespeare an entirely different light is thrown on the text. Elgar called *Falstaff* a symphonic study, presumably meaning that through the medium of music he was making a review of his subject, much as a Hazlitt makes one in prose. He was proud of his *Falstaff* and actually wrote his own analysis of the score. And, bless his heart, what manner of man does he show us bearing the name of Falstaff? A Falstaff in C minor. Few of us would think of a Falstaff who 'accommodates' a minor key (as Bardolph says, 'accommodated; that is, when a man is, as they say, accommodated; or, when a man is, being, whereby a' may thought to be accommodated'). Few of us would dwell regretfully on Falstaff's misspent life and on the English gentleman he might have been. The dream in the orchard, in Elgar's tone-poem, is a tender miniature in the *Wand of Youth* vein; but is this the Falstaff who conquered life by gusto and wit, so that nobody believes he was cast out when the King passed him by? Banish Jack and banish all the world. Elgar creates Falstaff in his own image; fundamentally, like many great men, he was naive; Elgar's Falstaff has spent as much time in Worcester Cathedral blowing himself out with the singing of anthems as he has lying on benches after noon. The true hero of *Falstaff* is Prince Hal; Hal is the hero, not only dramatically, but because the patriotic note suited Elgar's musical style. The only broad rich theme in the work represents the Prince; and it is a theme which, with its leap of a seventh, recalls most of the basic themes in Elgar.

Elgar was an honest artist, without powers of dramatic deception. *Falstaff* is Elgar himself, devoted as much to austerity as to sack. *Gerontius* is Elgar too. The symphonic study presents a Falstaff turned fasting friar and one who has written an apologia for his life. Elgar could not get out of his own skin. The idea has been expressed by some of his admirers (of whom I certainly am one, second to none other) that Elgar could have written an opera. Doubts arise about this speculation as soon as we consider the scant amount of sensuous beauty given to the women in *Falstaff*. Elgar's music contains no sex appeal; certainly his muse could not descend to the state of Doll Tearsheet and such.

The finest pages in the *Falstaff* score occur where Elgar sets Falstaff against a background of historical pomp and circumstance; where, for example, the crowd swarms to see the procession; the accumulating hubbub is splendidly done, the tiptoe craning-of-the-neck expectancy; and there is the exact moment when the King comes into view. The orchard episode is fragrant with Gloucestershire at the time of the ripening of the pippin: the music sounds the rustic tabor; and muted strings penetrate to the core of Shakespeare's 'Now comes in the sweet o' th' night'. I myself wish for no music more national than this. And of course as craftsmanship *Falstaff* is Elgar at his most comprehensive. Elgar's mind was not witty; the sherris-sack of Falstaff did not ascend into Elgar's brain, making it full of nimble fiery and delectable shapes; this is an old-port Falstaff, conscious that he owest God a death; 'virtuously given as a gentleman need to be; virtuous enough; swore little; diced not above seven times a week; went to a bawdy house not above once a quarter ... of an hour'. Verdi, in his old age, was truer to Falstaff, for though he began from the buffoon of *The Merry Wives of Windsor*, he transcended his theme and embraced the magnificent old scamp and sophist who asked if honour could set to a leg.

The essence of Elgar is in *Gerontius* and the 'Enigma' Variations. The austere dweller in the cloister and the man of out-of-doors. *Gerontius* is in no single bar of the score unfaithful to the general portrait I have tried to draw of Elgar – the sane Elgar, human to the point of perpetual companionability. There is no abnormality in Elgar's portrayal of man's dread of death; this Gerontius is no

finely spiritual ascetic burning a Palestrina flame; he is a
human being. No Palestrina provides the agony of Gerontius; the echo of Amfortas is a masterstroke. The work is
original; to this day we can feel the boldness of Elgar; he
took the form of an oratorio of his period and filled it with
a surging unreticent orchestra which actually borrowed the
leading-motif principle from Wagner. Nobody except Elgar
could have written *Gerontius*; it is not, by the way, an
oratorio, only an adaptation of oratorio style to a more
personal end. The poem of Cardinal Newman was as a
rock that had to be struck by the rod of music before the
heart of it was awakened. The remarkable fact is that
Elgar was most times clumsy and unsympathetic in his
handling of words, yet in *Gerontius* there are many
felicities of accentuation and of phrasing; for example the
reiterated notes at the words 'I went to sleep', followed by
the rise to F natural on 'strange' in the phrase 'a strange
refreshment'. Inspiration runs through Part I; the semi-
chorus was, I think, an invention of Elgar's own, and with
fine instinct for atmosphere and dramatic perspective he
uses his voices to waft to the upper air the prayers on earth
for the soul of Gerontius. The wonder of the hush that is
in the music at the words 'How still it is; I hear no more
the busy beat of Time' never fails to enthral the imagination; and where is there a more impassioned musical
evocation of the sense of dissolution – 'this emptying out of
each constituent'? At this point, the music *is* the sound of
some essence running away into nothingness.

I am not an uncritical admirer of Elgar; I have in this
essay tried to point out a few of his shortcomings, as I feel
them. I certainly am not prejudiced in Elgar's favour by
his main religious and intellectual points of view. I am, as
the Hyde Park orator said, 'an atheist, thank God!' I loathe
the Kipling-cum-Joseph Chamberlain imperialism which

Elgar often seems to extol. *Gerontius* to me is nothing but a work of art. I am considering here the music strictly as music composed as a setting to a poem. To deny its individuality and the easy mastery of the means of expression is a sign of insensibility or want of acquaintance with the score. *Gerontius* is one of the few choral works which are imaginative in a personal way. Its appearance amongst the oratorios of England of forty years ago was one of the surprises of music's history. From land so barren no other composer has produced a fruit of half this richness.

At one point only does Elgar fail in *Gerontius*, and the failure illustrates my notion of him as an honest artist who had nothing of the actor in him. He can do nothing much with the Demons. Strauss, in a letter to Hofmannsthal, confesses that he cannot find the right music for Joseph (in *Josephlegende*) because 'there is no strain of piety in my family'. Elgar could be pious or devout with the best of them but he did not have an ounce of the demonic in him. His devils, in *Gerontius*, are even more gentlemanly than Milton's Lucifer is noble. But much too much fuss has been made of Elgar's inability to express Satanism – the demonic element in *Gerontius* is episodic and incidental; the work is great where it had to be great. The contrasted drama and 'transfiguration' (no Straussian Christmas-card view of Heaven here!); the change from the chill at heart of Part I to the timeless quietness of Part II – Elgar was at liberty while composing these pages to strike the table, like Thackeray, and cry out: 'By God, genius!'

In the 'Enigma' Variations we find Elgar the man of the world of sane human relationships; he depicts himself amongst his friends in his most original orchestral work. Here is the Elgar known by the few who were allowed to get near him; the Elgar who loved to go to the Hereford Club in Festival time and learn (immediately after a

performance of *Gerontius*, maybe) what horse had won the
St Leger, and at what price; the Elgar who could be
boisterous and boyish; who could enjoy the pretty lisp of a
charming woman (the 'Dorabella' string delicacy of stress
and figuration); the Elgar who laughed at his dog battling
ashore in the River Wye; the Elgar who walked the
meadows in the sunset talking of a Beethoven slow movement; the Elgar who loved to don his knee-breeches and
put on all his decorations. As portraiture at one and
the same time intimately subjective and intimately
objective, sensitive and tender and vigorous and meditative
in turn, the 'Enigma' set can go confidently into the
choicest of music's portrait galleries. The 'Nimrod' adagio
is a slow movement of noble carriage, rising to a crescendo of
imposing rhetoric, followed by a diminuendo which has few
superiors as an expression of benedictory emotion; the 'cello
variation is beautifully felt in its long winding phrases; and
the 'Romanza' is a seascape conceived and presented with
the highest imaginative art; the music is visual. The lovely
swaying wood-wind figure waves goodbye; the throb of the
liner is heard; and the quotation from Mendelssohn grows
fainter; the variation is adorable in its affection, fancy and
many felicities of orchestral technique. The 'Enigma'
Variations contain the best that was in Elgar. The symphonies reveal Elgar the laureate. In these two works the
private poet of the 'Enigma' Variations, of the 'cello
concerto and the slow movement of the Violin Concerto,
puts on his ceremonial robes and achieves the self-conscious
orchestral apotheosis. The A flat Symphony extols Church
and State; the E flat Symphony, not so obviously *nobilimente*,
and technically not as varied and interesting, strikes a less
ceremonial note in the glowing fourth movement, which
opens with something of the heartswelling fullness of
harmony of the beginning of the finale of the 'St Antony'

Variations of Brahms. The cadence at the end where the 'motto' theme falls in reflective sequence and the orchestra burgeons in a quick crescendo, gives the lie to the charge of complacency occasionally urged against Elgar.

In the symphonies, Elgar does not bind himself to the wheel of cyclic development; the First Symphony, in particular, shows him transforming the germ motif almost improvisatorily, or garlanding it with subsidiary themes. One of the A flat Symphony's most arresting points, in fact, is its improvisations of texture and rhythm, the music turns upon itself down many a labyrinthine way, discovers bypaths of quiet thought, shoots up unexpected and rich growths from the main structure. It is in the symphonies where we come repeatedly upon Elgar's curious dualism of temperament; he is, as I say, mainly the laureate in the symphonies, inclined to strike the official attitude and address us in blank-verse. At other times, he retires from the public view, forgets Whitehall and Westminster and the cathedral cities; unannounced stillnesses come over the symphonies, strange fallings away from pageantry; then the music is sweetened by the moods of the other and different Elgar. The vaulted melodies of the First Symphony's adagio die down to a silence that seems to hold the heart of peace beating somewhere. The use of muted trombones and horns at the end of this adagio; the colour obtained by string divisions in both of the symphonies; the subtle carrying over of the triple rhythm from the first movement to the larghetto of the E flat Symphony; the extension of cadenza style in the Violin Concerto – these may be quoted as amongst the more palpable instances of how Elgar drew into the crucible of his imagination an inherited technique. The rondo of the Second Symphony is evidence in itself of Elgar's power to invest a familiar musical style with an entirely new feeling and colour; an unexpected transformation of a lofty theme from the first movement, now grotesque, struggles through a crescendo of drum-beats with the orchestra palpitating in every part: the passage is as dramatic and inexplicable as the great pedal-point episode in the first movement of Mahler's Ninth Symphony ('wie eine Kondukt').

He pointed no new direction. If he had never composed a note, there would be today no link missing from the main evolution of the vocabulary and syntax of music. For this reason the new Aesthetic has little use for him. Moreover, he is deemed with Wagner, Brahms and others, terribly and romantically bourgeois. As I have argued above, I see no reason why an artist is under the necessity to forge fresh forms of expression if he can find at his hand an organized and suggestive language, one that he can instinctively learn and speak. The present age inclines to a scientific, not an aesthetic interest in art. I can see that an astronomer is more or less obliged to discover a new star from time to time if he wishes to rank with the greatest of his order. A composer of genius, even of talent, deserves estimation by a less prosaic measure.

Elgar 'invented' nothing, no doubt; like the noble lord in the Goldoni play, he lets us know that a gentleman is at home in all countries. Yet in spite of all temptations to belong to other nations, he remained an Englishman. He was born in the West of England, and he lies buried in the shadow of the Malvern Hills. He showed us all that was lovely in English life; that is why English folk cherish his music, for all its faults; sometimes because of them.

x

Delius
1863-1934

Delius

I⊤ is interesting sometimes to study composers cheek by jowl, not of course to weigh one against the other but to throw into prominence by contrast the characteristic points of each. The difference between Delius and Elgar may be emphasized by two words which, though superficially they mean the same thing, mark a pretty distinction. Elgar is the laureate most times. Delius the poet always. There is, as we have seen in the preceding chapter, usually a touch of the ceremonial in Elgar's music; it is either Opening or Closing something. Elgar's emotion is frequently a public, not a private emotion. When the Second Symphony of Elgar comes to an end with a swell of the orchestra followed by a decrescendo and falling sequences of melody, I think of Whitehall seen on a summer evening from the old bridge of St James's Park, a scene proud and self-consciously English, beautiful but too substantial to be poetic.

There are no State Occasions in the music of Delius, no emotion that is not personal and intimate, no beauty that is not thin-spun and touched with the sense of brevity. Delius usually stands apart from the world. Even in *Brigg Fair*, for example, the flesh-and-blood jollity of countryside revels is left out; the mnsic tells only of the bloom that was once on the hour. With Elgar emotion is tangible more often than not, and, so to say, contemporary. Delius recollects emotion in tranquillity. I do not suggest – as most of Delius's critics mistakenly do suggest – that he lacks the power of climax and is without masculinity. I shall

presently show that Delius was by no means the 'escapist' of
his legend; that, on the contrary, he was an artist of a wide
range of ideas and emotions; and that compared with him
most English-speaking composers of his day were parochial
and merely gentlemanly. But the point to be emphasized at
once in any appreciation of Delius is that in all his humours
and moods the technique and the stuff of his art were pure
poetry; he drew everything, his dreams and the energies of
his waking active life, through one of the finest sensibilities
music has known in our time. In *Brigg Fair* there is a
climax of such passion and strength that most other climaxes
in English music of Delius's period seem to me as though
mechanically hoisted up by pulleys. I refer to the passage
which occurs just before the main melody is transferred to
trumpets and trombones (*con solennita*); where the strings
swirl in winding abounding phrases – one of the very few
climaxes in nineteenth-century orchestral music that is not
wholly dependent on the trick of accumulation by
sequences. But even here Delius does not give us a present
or active exultation; it is too rapt for that. This emotion
has been purified by reflectiveness; the reality has
already become remote. Delius is usually reminding us
that poetry is what is left to us after the show of life has
passed on.

We shall perhaps begin our study of Delius best by an
analysis of the technical means whereby he obtains his
effects; with artists as poetic as Delius we must keep our
eye severely on music as music, on the methods of composition. We are free to write as eloquently as maybe of
his poetry only if first of all we give some guarantee that
we have listened to him with ears strictly concerned about
music. Delius has been unfortunate in his critics; they have
praised him for his sensibility and what-not; and invariably
they have left out his music – his art – in the dithyrambs of

their adoration. He must often have prayed for deliverance from the Delians, as Debussy prayed for deliverance from the Debussyites.

II

In music, more than in any other of the arts, legends and fallacies arise rapidly and can only with difficulty be knocked on the head. The reason lies in the nature of music, in its insubstantiality and most of all in its dependence for existence on a performance. Few people really know a composition in the intimate way that they know a poem or a picture or a piece of prose. Few people know the language of music; score-reading is a rare accomplishment even amongst musicians, and it takes us no closer to the reality of the work than the ordnance survey takes an expert map reader to the living shape and substance and encompassing light and air of a place, city, district or countryside.

Only by some such reasoning can I account for the perpetual dissemination of misleading opinions about music and composers, the equal of which in stupidity could not possibly occur in the criticism of the other arts. Brahms was once thought by the majority of musicians to be a drab and academic writer for the orchestra; Mahler has been linked with Beethoven in style and in his thought-processes; Verdi was in his day accused of Wagnerisms; Ravel was actually thought to resemble Debussy in matters of essential style. Most peculiar of all errors is that which describes Delius as a sort of dilettante composer, as an imaginative amateur, vague of feeling and capable of exquisite suggestions; but a poor musician. He was certainly not always expert in his scoring for orchestra, but all the same he usually got into his canvas what he wanted. Every composer, so far as he is a realized artist, commands as much technique as his conceptions need. It is beyond belief – or it would be beyond belief in a less hurried and scatter-minded world than ours – that Delius is nowadays accepted by nine musicians out of every ten as a composer of the order called 'atmospheric'; which, of course, damns him as one who possessed little or no strict musical resource. The fact is there for all to ponder, who will take the trouble, that two of Delius's finest works are written in variation-form. As variation-form and nothing else, 'Appalachia' and *Brigg Fair* will survive tolerant scrutiny; the changes through which Delius puts the slave-theme in 'Appalachia'; the devices of melodic and rhythmic and harmonic transformations, the freedom of counterpoint, the divisions and placings of string and vocal parts; here is ample resource of technique, indeed we have only to make a catalogue of the various devices which usually pass for signs of an academic culture to realize how puerile it is to suggest that any of these formulae were beyond the scope of Delius. If Professor Donald Tovey could have composed a mirror-fugue almost more complicated and erudite than any other in existence, would it have signified as evidence either for or against the Professor's, or anybody else's gifts as an artist?

It is the commonest of errors of criticism to make a distinction between an artist and his technique; to consider that his way of expression can be studied in the abstract as a thing apart from what has been expressed. When I was very young, dons of literature sometimes deplored that Charles Dickens lacked the polished art of Thackeray; in a word, they thought that if Dickens had written differently, a greater Dickens he would have been. Our only concern with any artist is first his originality and, after that, whether he has something to say that is worth while. He need not soar to the heights; he is not under an obligation to measure himself with the greatest. Delius is not a Beethoven or – to approximate closer to his category – he is not a Debussy. But he is himself, and for many of us he is unique and valuable as one artist amongst many who make life worth living. In what way could this music, which we know at once as an emanation from the sensibility of Delius, have been composed other than in the way chosen by Delius and have remained true to the man? We are free to question an artist's way of expression when obviously there is a discrepancy between the imaginative conception and the produced work. We may, for example, look dubiously into much of the chamber music of Delius; for here the idea is not realized in a natural and convincing way. We feel that Delius is unhappy when he is working in the so-called classical forms, that he is wasting material which he might have used to better purpose. It is in his chamber music that Delius really is the amateur. Yet even here there are the proofs of his genius; a technically unsatisfactory string quartet by a Delius is more interesting than one immaculately fabricated by the next doctor of music.

Delius failed in his chamber music for much the same reason that Debussy failed to make his G minor Quartet consistently engrossing. He conceived music more in terms of mood and sensibility than in terms of contrasted ideas; in other words, he was happier with colours than with black and white lines. But we must not carry this generalization too far; it is untrue to say that Delius possessed no linear sense or little feeling for symmetry or transition of theme. It is not given to a 'colourist', an impressionist working only in timbres and orchestral chiaroscuro, to compose variations as satisfying *as variations* as the 'Appalachia' set and *Brigg Fair*. Delius needed an emotion of poetry to move him to composition; he turned naturally to the orchestra and to blended voices. He was a painter more than he was a draughtsman; but a painter has his severe logic of form. I protest against the common notion that Delius at his finest was a meanderer; on the contrary, the form of works such as *In a Summer Garden*, 'Appalachia' and *Brigg Fair* is clear, relevant in every phrase, and rounded. A study of *In a Summer Garden* will reveal a melodic sequence of the nicest consequentiality; the development is from within; compared with the form of *In a Summer Garden* I suggest that the sonata-form of the academies is as the square four-legged carpentry of a table to the free and various and balanced growth of a tree. Like Debussy in *L'Après-midi d'un Faune*, Delius creates a musical shape of his own for his orchestral pieces; but he does not, contrary to general belief, proceed as Debussy does from floating and expanding harmony. Delius's texture is invariably linked to a melodic line; I know of few places in the music of Delius where there is not a definite melodic appeal. Yet Delius has been labelled 'atmospheric', a composer in vague washes of harmony; he has thus been tied up and labelled and put neatly away in the pigeon-holes of the encyclopaedias. I wonder sometimes whether many people in the world really listen to music and ever get to know it.

III

It is, Busoni said, the forms of music that survive; and form in music is crystallized thought. The finer the art the more likely is it to interest ages to come, and survive the changeful whims of the Zeitgeist. *Tristan* lives today because of its organized music; the Schopenhauerisms are of no consequence whatever. Strauss's *Also sprach Zarathustra* enjoyed a brief life on the strength of the vogue of Nietzsche's Superman, now as extinct as the dodo. Strauss's music in this work lacks vital form or organization; therefore it lies buried with the philosophy that inspired it. (But Nietzsche's poem outlives the philosophy because of its art, as poetry.)

I think Delius will endure for a long time to come by virtue of his sensibility and his complete mastery of as much of technique as he needed. First of all let us look into the structure or physiology of one or two characteristic works of Delius; if we find a sound constitution and cerebellum we may with some assurance count upon a reasonable longevity.

The 'Appalachia' Variations were sketched in 1897 and completed in 1902, a period during which nearly every British composer was churning out music more or less Teutonic in its square rhythms and excessive orchestration. Delius employs variation-form in 'Appalachia' with a musicianship demonstrable in every bar, but he adapts the variation-form to his own imaginative ends and departs entirely from precedent. Every other set of orchestral variations, as far as I can recollect, begins with a statement of the theme which is to be varied. Delius prepares the stage for his theme, which he uses as a dramatic motif representing the enslaved people. He begins the work with a long introduction; a tone-poem evoking the sense of lonely vacant nature; a horn-call is sounded, and it is the main theme in embryo or as though echoed far away. Delius quotes from this introduction for poetic effect later in the course of the variations, and each variation carries the psychological interest a stage farther.

Considered strictly as variations of theme and harmony and orchestral colour, 'Appalachia' is of engrossing musical interest. The theme itself has been recognized as having something in common with the first phrase of the quartet in *Rigoletto*, no great scholarship or insight are needed to point the surface resemblance. Where, in the St Antony Variations of Brahms, or in the Mozart Variations of Reger, or in the Symphonic Variations of Dvořák, or in any other orchestral variations, can we find a transition, a building up from a simple foundation to a noble arch more imaginatively musical than Delius's transition from his slave-theme to the *molto lento* and its solemn processional tread and its muffled drums, and the descent of the brass before we reach this *molto lento*. Then, at the end of the lamentation, Delius modulates gently to eight vocal parts at the words:

... After night has gone comes the day.

Only the highest order of inspiration can work as simply as this. It is strong music, tender music, majestic music and music aching with the Delius nostalgia. Also it is music fashioned with personal and self-contained craftsmanship. Delius's treatment of voices in 'Appalachia' is his own; here, by the way, is another original stroke – no other set of variations calls for a chorus. Delius does not give us the voices in full at once, just as he does not give us his main theme in full at once. He is never obvious; he is as far removed from the obvious as Debussy himself. Long before the voices take concrete shape we hear only suggestions of them. The weaving of vocal echoes into the general texture of tone is delicate and haunting; for example, the end of the fourth and fifth variations may be quoted. From the point of view of fine musical craftsmanship and fine musical thinking; from the point of view of intensely imaginative expression, 'Appalachia' is a masterpiece over which is suffused a beauty so slender that it catches us suddenly and inexplicably by the throat. Yet with all its ache of sensibility, the music goes through masculine and even rough weather before it dies away into the mists which concealed the secret places of the heart of the most poetic composer born in England.

In *Brigg Fair* Delius makes an entirely different use of variation-form; in 'Appalachia' the theme is a starting-point, a fragment to be developed and enlarged; a dramatic motif signifying the ache for liberation. Delius puts his slave-theme through psychological as well as musical changes. In *Brigg Fair*, on the other hand, there is no drama, no psychological transition; it is a nature piece recollected in passionate tranquillity. The changes or variations are not dynamic or dramatic; they are variations of subjective emotion or poetry. And so Delius employs a variation technique at the extreme to the variation technique employed in 'Appalachia'. The main theme of *Brigg Fair* is complete as an organized melody when it is first announced at the outset of the work; nature goes through no crises that are not implicit in herself from the beginning; Delius with one rapt caress of the orchestra creates his remembered universe, poised at high noon and still as the hour-glass; here is the breath and soul of landscape in England, misty to the earth's end; a country scene with a lark singing and a poet overhearing. Where is there music more passionate than this? And Delius has been included amongst the emotional weaklings and exhibitionists, with a perpetual chromatic whine and little manliness! The world likes to think of drama as an external process in which physical passion spins the plot; violence and visible kinetic motion are now definitely needed as proof of virility in an artist. Legends multiply in an age of hasty living and hasty reading. No good was done to the cause of Delius by the perpetuation of portraits painted of him in his old age, when he was blind and paralysed and wasted by ravages of a life lived recklessly enough.[1] The public mind grasps at an image and forms its views on most things like the savage who has not outgrown the pictographic method of expressing

[1] 'It is deplorable that these portraits were ever allowed to be published, for they have created in the public mind a legendary figure of the man ... though there was lovableness and a certain charm, the chief trait in my collected impression of the man is his severity ... a man of whom Nietzsche would have said "Here is one of the great despisers" ... ' *Delius as I Knew Him*, by Eric Fenby, p. 191.

concepts. There is ample power of imagination and strong musical fibre in the *Mass of Life* and *The Village Romeo and Juliet*; one of the main traits of Delius's style, in fact, is the recurrent uncouthness of his writing for the brass, a trait not to be accounted for by want of knowledge of 'how to score'. An artist expresses himself without inhibitions, within the limitations of his medium; his only responsibility is to his style. Delius was on the whole a water-colourist of music, not a filler of big canvasses with oils, though as I have said, the *Mass of Life* is a large-spanned work. In terms of his instinctively chosen and developed style, Delius composed true to most of his moods; we must not be put off the scent of the full man that he was; poetry can be stern and even rough. Swinburne once was abused by the driver of a hansom cab; he had tendered the legal fare and no more. Swinburne listened for a while to the driver's expletives, then said: 'Come down from your —— —! box and hear how a poet can swear.' Delius does not exactly make his music utter round oaths, but it is not all sensibility pure and undefiled.

Chromatic harmony was his natural element. We are free to take exception to an artist's means of expression only when style mechanically hardens into mannerism; and instead of the gesture that is spontaneous and significant we are given only a sort of fussy meaningless twiddling of a button or a fidgeting with a paper-knife; the sort of mannerism which in Madame de Staël nearly drove Schiller crazy. Every composer now and again lapses into formulae or mere habit, when inspiration burns feebly the machine creaks and obtrudes – Wagner and his sequences; dotted crotchet and quaver and two-bar phrases in Elgar; the thrum-thrum of Sibelius's strings with the wood-wind and brass's sharp ejaculation in the background; major and minor modulations in Schubert; the block harmony of

Schumann – they show the tricks of the trade overmuch at times, the greatest as well as the smallest. All art is compact of devices, and the highest order of genius is required always to keep the wires and filaments charged with the current of imagination. Delius frequently is chromatic and little else; style weakens to mannerism.

Let us return to a consideration of Delius at his best. We were discussing structure in his music. His use of variation-form was, as we have seen, flexible; the technical procedure was governed by the poetic idea. Delius less than most composers fitted himself to a Procrustean bed. In much music we come to a point where we can see where the form was consciously occupying the composer's attention as he wrote; it was a scaffolding set up in advance of the act of creation. In many important places in Brahms you can catch the formalist at work, spanning more or less skilfully the vacant spaces of the imaginative terrain. Delius also twiddles his thumbs here and there; but not in any of his representative works. *In a Summer Garden* is, let me suggest again, a most felicitous example of inevitable growth into shapeliness, phrase blossoming from phrase as naturally as the flowers and trees in the scene which inspired the work. This is no ornamental garden, with plots and beds and lawns artificially laid out; it is a garden of lovely fresh and abundant blooms which make their order by grace of the law of nature's own poise. There are definite themes, even long-phrased melodies, and they are developed and diversified with a sure and happy touch; the melodiousness of *In a Summer Garden* is such, that for all its harmonic implications and its importance as texture, it can be sung or whistled throughout; even when the harmonies move and modulate without apparent regard for a tonal centre, the melodic contours are never seriously imperilled. I can think of only two other orchestral pieces where the connection of theme and orchestral tissue and movement onward are as original, as instinctive, and as inevitable, without resort to the usual and definable charts of known musical anatomy, as they are in the *Summer Garden*; these pieces are *L'Après-midi d'un Faune* and the 'Siegfried' Idyll.

Delius has been accused of a lack of counterpoint. The composer-poet does not need counterpoint – which is more necessary for the firm prose rather than for the volatile poetry of music. Though Delius has melody enough, it is never of the kind that could be more than half suggested in a series of statements or subjects; it is the product of his style of harmony, not the source of it. Melody which can be treated contrapuntally must exist in itself; it is a cause and not an effect of harmony. In Delius, as in Debussy, melody is the flower and harmony the soil – or (as this is a heavy metaphor) the harmony is the translucent water and the melody the lovely play of light upon it. The texture of Delius's music is not by any means without an interest of polyphony – but it is a polyphony not of notes but of chords. There is in Delius a balance of melody and harmony so even, a mingling of line and colour so subtle that it is hard to say where the one ends and the other begins. If the rhythm is here and there a little monotonous this is a price which the composer had to pay; as I pointed out in my chapter on Debussy, rhythmical interest is inevitably bound to go into the background in a pre-occupation with harmonic colour and expansion. In any case there is rhythm and rhythm. The common view of rhythm in music is palpable stresses which can be measured in groups of notes. Stravinsky's *Le Sacre du Printemps* is popularly supposed to be a masterpiece of rhythm. For my own part I find *Le Sacre du Printemps* much an affair of accentuation; a marvellous exploitation of primitive rum-ti-tum. The rhythm of Delius is a flowing and

interchanging of tonal currents; it is like a rhythm of changing light; it is not the rhythm of a solid but of an essence.
And it takes no shape or form except the shape and form
instinctively chosen by Delius, as the music was wakened in
him by no prompting in the world except that of his own
feeling. But the people who cannot see form and balanced
growth in Delius are as people who admire best the wired rose.

IV

A genius of course does what he chooses; he himself
discovers the laws that govern the constitution of his art.
Then the pedants come along and abstract from works of
art already created a table of abstract commandments to
which they expect all other artists, some of them still
unborn, to conform. No two artists have observed the same
procedure in form, style, technique; grammar is usually
transcended by the next genius – who leaves the observance
of it to the scruples of men who have nothing original to
say. An artist is valuable in so far as he makes a contribution.
It is not necessary for all geniuses to comprehend life in all
its fullness and diversity. The greatest of them are rapid
and comprehensive in their vision and feelings; artists such
as Mozart and Shakespeare possess those 'large general
powers' which Dr Johnson expected to find in the highest of
geniuses. There is another and lower order of genius which
at its least commanding and universal achieves a higher
order of creative power than ever comes within the scope of
the genius who is only a man of action. The poet inten-
sifies the feeling for beauty; and beauty is the only endurable
truth; it has nothing to do with the things that sooner or
later must perish because they are conditioned by temporal
and accidental laws of change. A work of art does not
necessarily decay because it lacks what we call science,

scholarship, law, logic. Giotto knew little or nothing of the 'laws' of perspective. Stanford was a more sophisticated and better-informed composer than Mussorgsky. Genius is a miracle. Delius composed original works; there is nothing in existence at all like his opera *The Village Romeo and Juliet*; from the only example of this work known to the general public we can learn at once of an original mind and style, and of a melody and a harmony that come from a unique sensibility.

There is another delusion about Delius which is the consequence of the error of expecting one artist to follow the procedure of any other. It is said that Delius could not write for voices. The trouble apparently is that he often disregarded the stress and accent of his verbal text. Here is a delusion which has been perpetuated by the rationalist school of musical criticism. There is no reason at all why a composer in setting words should reproduce in his music every accentuation. The rhythm of music, the stresses of music, are different from those of verse. When a composer writes for voices he does not supply merely incidental music to words; he takes the poet into his own world, where the laws of rhythm and pulsation are entirely different. A song belongs to music; it is not a recitation in which the poet is as important as the composer. It is the prosiest view of vocal music that it must needs wait on the rhythm and accentuation of words. If the composer can fit into his scheme the stresses of verse, well and good; but usually the vocal composer who does honour and recognize every syllable and accentuation in the poet's discourse is not one whose mind is wholly alive with warm impulsive music. If Wolf had been as consistently and as utterly inspired by music as Schubert, he could not have attended as conscientiously as he did to the pure prosody values of his poets. Delius put some of his finest conceptions into the forms of vocal music;

his opera *The Village Romeo and Juliet*; the *Mass of Life*, *Sea Drift*; and 'Appalachia'. To say that he could not write felicitously for solo voice is a statement which can be revealed as nonsense by a reference simply to one or two bars of the solo music in *Sea Drift*; did Hugo Wolf himself scan a verbal phrase more beautifully, with more poetic consideration, than Delius's treatment of Whitman's words:

And every day I, a curious boy, never too close, never
  disturbing them,
Cautiously peering, absorbing, translating.

This is only one example: the reader will find for himself in *Sea Drift* ample places where words and music are mated with the aptness of love and delight. Far from the truth is it that Delius could not compose vocal music; on the contrary, the *Mass of Life* contains some of the most beautiful of all music written for massed voices. It is because Delius declined to tie his music down to the stresses and everyday significance of words that he is the only composer, with the exception of Debussy, who has given us a choral style that is not oratorical, not emphatic and square and prosy; but instead a choral style which mingles with music's own immaterial sensuousness the pulsations and colours of voices, blending them into the general texture, evocative and not prosily verbal. Choral singers in Delius should be heard – not seen.

Half a year ago I happened to find myself deep in study of music written in styles and periods at the extreme to those associated with Delius; I was long absorbed in works mainly contrapuntal and classical. With a shock I returned to the *Mass of Life* to find as I thought and felt (but not for long) that it had a monotonous and loosely connected melodic and harmonic sequence, and a certain fatal clumsiness of technique. I had known, of course, that Delius

never in his long life composed with professional slickness;
but in this mood of reaction his 'faults' stuck out miles. I
feared that I was about to share the fate of Philip Heseltine,
whose enthusiastic admiration of Delius turned in time
almost to loathing the mere sound of the man's music. In
this mood of uncertainty, for well do I know that Delius is
very much a matter of taste, I chanced to come upon a
notice written a few years ago by one of the more distinguished of our younger critics. It deals with the famous
performance at the Albert Hall in London when Sir
Thomas Beecham engaged Fischer-Dieskau to sing the
baritone solos. This notice was in no doubt at all about the
Mass of Life's bad points –

> ... yet the demand would scarcely warrant more
> frequent performances, nor is it heresy to say the same
> of the work itself, for even the composer's disciples do
> not regard it as one of his best. The solemn, naive
> philosophy selected from Nietzsche's *Also sprach
> Zarathustra* is even more distant from our present
> mentality and more irrelevant to the spiritual problems
> of our age than that of the composer's other poet, Walt
> Whitman. And Delius has done nothing to make it
> more palatable. He gives the music neither symphonic
> continuity and concentration, such as one finds, say,
> in Beethoven's Mass in D, nor variety of texture and
> colour, such as one finds in Britten's 'Spring'
> Symphony.

For a while, even these severe charges against the *Mass
of Life* did not outrage me, though, of course, I at once
disregarded the nonsense to the effect that even the composer's disciples cannot count the *Mass* as one of his
greatest. On the contrary, they regard it as his masterpiece.
(So did Delius himself.) Heseltine's opinion of it at one time

was almost certifiable – 'this colossal work, without doubt the greatest musical achievement since Wagner, a Mass worthy to rank beside the great Mass of Sebastian Bach ...' And Cecil Gray thought that, in the *Mass*, Delius makes us feel conscious that 'he is putting forth his full strength'. But the young contemporary critic's main castigations seemed to me not without foundations – in the non-Delian mood in which chance had thrown me. It is a conceit of our period that critics can perpetually rise above the subjective state, achieving Olympian objectivity. I do not believe it. Critical opinions sometimes are not intellectually made or organized; 'they just grow'. It is seldom that we hear of a change of mind in a professional music-critic; he sticks in 1956 mainly to what he told his constituency in 1930. Consistency in abstract opinions is easy to sustain; consistency in good taste involves long experience. Critical belief, like religion and love, should be able to cope with temporary infidelities.

Absorption in music at all contrapuntal or linear is really a bad way of preparing to listen to Delius; we might as well eat fish with red wine – and I hope soon to show that the music of Delius is by no means all Sauterne. Counterpoint and the so-called classical patterns can't encourage expression of personal emotion; and Delius used music entirely to express himself as poet. He was first a poet and second a musician. And as there are poets who choose words not for their dictionary meanings, so there are one or two composers who choose tones and arrange them not for strictly musical purposes. Delius was the most independent of composers in style and aesthetics; as a man, too, he remained apart from the schools, fashions, 'tendencies'.

My return to Delius was made with my critical antennae so much on guard that the familiar defects in Delius – flaccid, repetitive rhythms, the same limited chromatic harmony, the persistent horn and wood-wind cadences; in fact, all the Delian fingerprints – could be taken for granted much as we take for granted the sometimes tiresome characteristics of an old friend whom we haven't seen for some years. But soon the spell worked again; and this time, from a critical attitude which I think might have made mincemeat of all composers who have written anything recently, Delius emerged larger of stature than ever before, with a subtlety of diction in his vocal writing not to be immediately appreciated. It is in fact commonly thought, even by admirers of Delius, that the composer was usually careless about the way he treated words. In Eric Fenby's book *Delius as I Knew Him* (as fascinating at a tenth as at a first reading) we are told that Delius regarded voices as a necessary encumbrance, and that what he did understand 'was the colour of choral sounds'. In the *Mass of Life* words for solo voice are treated with a beauty and sensitiveness of musical – strictly musical! – inflexion scarcely to be surpassed by any composer of English birth, extraction or family association. Nietzsche's *Also sprach Zarathustra* obsessed Delius – and of course he is not concerned with his 'naive philosophy', but with the evocative power in the words. As examples of felicitous settings of words to music that draw the heart of significance and sound out of them, I will quote from the contralto's 'O Zarathustra' appeal, in Part I, especially at the line 'Wir zwei allein'; from the soprano's air, also in Part I, especially the lovely rising interval on the word 'weinten'; all the 'Süsse Leier!' invocation of Zarathustra, especially to the line 'Ein rosenseliger brauner Goldweingeruch'. Want of space holds me from other evidences easily to be found in the *Mass of Life*, showing that if the conception he had in mind called for sensitive musical poetic treatment of words Delius could compose vocal music with exquisite sense of verbal values. The falling cadences before the 'Come, it is the hour' of the

closing section, then the rising orchestra and the wonderful
simple modulation, and the sad, sustained notes of Zarathustra's 'Komm, lass' uns jetzt wandeln' and the world-
weary echo 'Nacht wandeln', are either great examples of
the fertilization of music by poetry – or some of us who
think so, including Sir Thomas Beecham, are musically
unfit to plead and are out of touch with contemporary
fashion.

The recurrent clumsiness and ineffectuality in Delius
were not the consequence of technical incompetence; his
distrust of academic *a priori* musical thinking was a mental
obsession. 'I've written pages of it myself,' he said to
Fenby, meaning cerebral or 'paper music', 'but I had the
sense to burn it. If you knew the amount of music I've
written and burned you'd be amazed. It is against my nature
to write music like that. The English like that sort of
thing....' And the Germans, too, he might have added. In
the *Mass of Life* certain awkward passages in the orchestration, the low pitch and stuffy spacing at the beginning of
the magical nocturne, for example, seem entirely wilful.
The tedious rhythmical emphasis during the 'Song of Life'
section is exasperating; the High School 'la-la'-ing of the
four-part girls' chorus in the 'Forest' section tests our
patience, except that every note obviously means much to
the composer, so that when he modulates – in the present
instance to the baritone meditation 'Die Sonne ist lange
schon hinunter' – we are richly compensated. The work is
certainly not without form or musical continuity, though I
would not go so far as to agree with Heseltine that its
'architecture' is 'majestical'. Four vibrant choruses pillar the
Mass from beginning to end; the rhapsodical periods are, so
to say, firmly columned. It is a mistake to suppose that
Delius was always a dreamy, nostalgic, reflective composer.
As a man, he lived a life which would have shocked, not to

say terrified, most of the musical toughs and Teddy Boys who nowadays belittle him as a romantic languisher. The strenuousness of the opening chorus of the *Mass* – 'O Du mein Wille!' – is absolutely apt to the purpose of expression. Will in Nietzsche was not asserted by grace; far from it. Only Strauss has equalled the triumphantly reckless brass writing of Delius in the orchestral accompaniment to these choruses. Maybe the burden or theme of the *Mass* is 'distant from our present mentality'; and may be it is none the worse for that.

V

The time will come, I think, when it will be understood that the kind of vocal music which sought to express words in all their dictionary significances will be regarded as a product of a period in the history of art when most minds were still incapable of functioning imaginatively without concrete supports from the so-called rational universe. I can never think without amazement that to this day the majority of musicians would describe the choral writing in the *Mass of Life* inferior *qua* choral writing to that of the *Missa Solennis* of Beethoven. The only poetic – that is to say, not verbally descriptive or didactic – choral music is by Delius, the only choral music that sings to us and does not assert or define. Debussy in 'La Damoiselle élue' came nearest to Delius's secret of drawing from massed human voices a music free of all the raw material of verbal utterance.

Delius was one of music's rare deviations from normal development – a 'sport', as the biologists say. In the nineteenth century he escaped, like Debussy, from the charted seas of music; he too found his island. But he was not, as Debussy was, enchanted out of the world by the magic of unexplored strands and seashore and rivers and woods, so that to him the sound of human sorrow came only as an echo, awakening no pain, no ache, only wonder and remembrance. Debussy was 'translated' into his own dreaming faun. Delius remained human and susceptible to the joys and pains he had known on the mainland. His music looks back on days intensely lived through; it knows the secret of the pathos of mortal things doomed to fade and vanish. At bottom Delius is pagan and epicurean. His music will never be familiar to a large crowd; and the few who have come to love it will try hard to keep it to themselves.

XI

Sibelius
1865-1957

Sibelius

THE history of the rise of Sibelius in the good opinion of the fashionable intelligence makes an interesting story. Forty or so years ago he was known in the parks, around the bandstands, as the composer of *Finlandia*; at concerts he was occasionally represented on the less austere evenings by the *Valse Triste*. Outside Finland a few musicians had studied the scores of the First and the Second of the symphonies, and the one in E minor was confidently supposed to be written in the manner and idiom of Tchaikovsky. Not until after the war of 1914-18 was Sibelius taken up by the best people of Great Britain and America; on the Continent in general his genius remained (and still remains) more or less unacknowledged or unrecognized. The remarkable fact is that the more bald and taciturn Sibelius's music became, the more and more his public grew in the places where it was played at all. The critics and the coteries of London were condescending about the First and the Second Symphonies, in which he exploits spacious tunes and strong and palpable and far-flung rhythms. It was only after Sibelius had absented himself from vulgarity a while; after he had pared his music down to the bone and adopted the aspect of aloof austerity that he interested the post-1918 leaders of what is what in the arts. Then the gramophone companies surprisingly ventured on his symphonies, all of them. Sibelius the swooning voluptuary of the *Valse Triste*; Sibelius the military-band rhetorician of *Finlandia*; and Sibelius the big-fisted and big-chested extrovert of the E minor Symphony, lived to see himself drawn in as a heavy reinforcement to aid the reaction against romanticism.

The climax of the Sibelius vogue was reached in London in 1938 when a festival conducted by Sir Thomas Beecham gave us a full-dress review, one after another, of the orchestral works. Audiences of the most distinguished pedigree attended Queen's Hall. The programme of the festival was of silk, with letters of gold; the 'patrons' seemed to exhaust Debrett. There were even testimonials (unsolicited) to the composer, including one from Bernard Shaw. As I turned over the pages I fully expected to come across: 'Mr —— (the promising young English composer) writes: "Seven years ago I heard Sibelius's music, since when I have written no other."' Some amount of instruction may be obtained from a discourse upon this strange case of Sibelius, his Metamorphosis and his Cult.

II

The Cult need not detain us long. New modes and new goods are always in demand in the Caledonian or Paddy's Market of the concert halls. 'Off with the old love and on with the new', said the forgotten Mr Dooley, 'and *off* with that'. The gramophone companies, as well as the virtuoso conductors here and there, needed a new line of business, a new discovery. (The symphonies of Sibelius, moreover, were short and compact enough to suit the prevailing technical scope of the recording rooms.) The general public liked this unwonted brevity in symphonic music; it was the age of the paragraph. There was also plenty of rhythm in Sibelius, another fact in his favour, for after 1918 rhythm came to be considered of more importance in music than any other constituent. Sibelius satisfied the demand in those places where music is as much a matter of going to concerts as it is a serious culture; he was 'modern' but not, like the atonalists, incomprehensible.

We can only guess of the comments made by Sibelius himself on his popularity, when the echoes of it reached him in the fastnesses of his home. Especially would it be instructive to know what he thought of the view, published by one or two critics in England, that he was in the line of Beethoven, bone of his bone, flesh of his flesh and spiritually attuned into the bargain. Later in this study I shall show that there are one or two formal characteristics of Sibelius which may be related to the Beethoven of the late quartets; there is no other resemblance, certainly not in one most crucial respect. In the music of Sibelius there is no ethical appeal. Sibelius is never concerned with the souls of mankind. He does not speak to the 'Umschlungenen Millionen'. His music does not even postulate an audience. We leave entirely the world of men and women and of ordinary values, moral and social, when we enter the world of Sibelius; we leave the pomp and circumstance and the sunlight, the enchanted islands and the disenchanted mainland. We leave, in fact, the temperate zone and get near to regions of thick-ribbed ice. Sibelius is neither classic nor romantic – as these terms are generally understood. He lacks the poise and serenity of the one, and he lacks the stains and dyes and odours of the other. He is at one and the same time the least objective and the least subjective of composers – which is perhaps so difficult a saying that I must try to elucidate. Sibelius does not express an individual emotion; he does not, to use Beethoven's phrase, speak from the heart to the heart; he does not express or suggest an ethic or a Weltanschauung. There are no fate-motifs in the music of Sibelius, no spiritual or psychological problems stated and conquered by the two-theme clash and resolution. The style is as distinctive as any of our day but it is impersonal in content. On the other hand, Sibelius is certainly not the objective artist who stands just a little back to portray or react impressionistically or pictorially in the manner of the Mussorgsky of *Night on the Bare Mountain*, or the Vaughan Williams of the 'Pastoral' Symphony, or the Arnold Bax of the Third Symphony. The music of Sibelius is as though the sights and sounds of his country, the air and the light and darkness, the legends and the history, had by some inner generative force become audible in terms of rustling violins, horn-calls out of a void, brass that swells to us in short gusts like music blown on a wind, beginning and ending almost as soon as heard; oboes and flutes that emit the clucking of weird fowl; bassoons that croak in the swamps and the mists. It is the music of animism. In Sibelius the forces of nature seem to live, move and have being of their own. During the course of my chapter on Wagner I write that he gave a tongue to the elements; but it was the tongue of histrionic utterance; fire and water and air and cloud are conscious powers in Wagner, working a human and superhuman destruction. Nature in Sibelius takes no cognizance of gods or of humans – certainly not of any intelligentsia, fashionable or other.

The world of Sibelius is unpeopled; there are no men and women in it, not a single living human being. The sedges are bare and no birds sing. Nobody loves and dies like a rose in aromatic pain. The scene and the drama of the music of Sibelius are nature; this, let me say once more, is the music of animism. The characters, the forces, the emotions expressed, are of the elements – wind and storm, the mists and night and dawn, the vacant landscape, the rustling grasses, the wailing of traditional ghosts, the menace of the dark and backward abysm. We hear the echo of old battles; and over everything Sibelius casts the dim light of legendary awe. Sibelius can exult, of course.

But it is not a man's high spirits that shake the orchestra
now, in sudden convulsions of tuba and brass; no mortal
flatulence could belch as the wood-wind of Sibelius belches;
and the ghostly endless whispering of Sibelius's violins as
they are driven along are not signs of an energy personal or
in the slightest volitional. Sibelius in the truest sense is a
national composer; I do not mean that at his greatest he is
ever regional or patriotic or political or that he uses folk-
songs. He is Finnish in the way that Wagner is German and
Elgar English. Mahler once said that he had 'already
composed the mountains of his homeland'. With much more
force could Sibelius claim to have set to music the landscape
of his country; for Mahler was much too autobiographical
to absorb himself in anything or anybody except Mahler
and his relation to his own and God's destiny. When
Sibelius turns his attention to men and women and mortal
passion – then it is that he commits the sentimentality of
the *salon*, as in the Romance in D flat, and the heap of
kindred rubbish that bears the signature of Jean Sibelius.
We need not, of course, think the less of Sibelius if he has
composed much second-rate and even familiar music; only
the smaller sorts of genius are constantly fastidious. Works
of the order of *Finlandia*, 'Rienzi' and the 'Pomp and
Circumstance' marches are signs not of a lack but an excess
of creative energy. I mention the banalities in Sibelius's
large output of music simply to support my point – they
were nearly all written when nature temporarily ceased to
compose for and through him. The paradox of it is that
though we may describe Sibelius as impersonal, aloof, and
withdrawn from the warm show of life, uninterested in the
ordinary theatre of our emotions and senses, none the less
he is the most masculine and fortifying composer of all
our contemporaries. Certainly he is the most original or, at
any rate, the most unlike any other. Not that he uses an

unfamiliar idiom or vocabulary; he makes no sound that would startle Beethoven, for example. Examine a score of Sibelius and you are at a loss to say at once exactly why the writing is original; the music is made of the familiar elements. Here, of course, is the true mark of originality; which does not mean an ability to turn the established order upside down – many clever young men can do that – but to give a fresh and individual turn or twist to the known language by virtue of a unique conception. Sibelius seems to compose out of the rawest of music's raw material. While his contemporaries have searched for a new synthesis (or however the latest jargon states it); while they have worn themselves dry with expense of grey matter to pronounce more and more cabalistic incantations wherewith to open the Aladdin's cave of music, coveting treasures of imagination not dreamed of before, all to be gathered in by utterance of the right and proper and latest spell, 'Abracadabra Polytonal: Abracadabra Atonal: Abracadabra Linear: Abracadabra Modal', Sibelius has been content to travel along the old well-trodden path; he has actually built his symphonic edifices out of the merest sticks and stones picked up on the main highway of music. The least imposing stuff suits his purposes – simple scale-passages, tiny nuclei of thirds in wood-wind, violin thrummings and spasmodic pizzicato; sudden interruptions from brass in one or two chords, followed by a weak echo from flutes, bassoons, oboes; barupt changes from rough accents to sustained harmonies; mists of string tone turned to a gold of trombone crescendi.

Sibelius is puzzling at first not because of the language he uses but by his ways of musical thinking. He is often elliptical; he leaves out unnecessary clauses; he composes mainly in nouns and verbs, with eloquent dashes of silence. He is a kind of musical Jack Bunsby. Even in his earliest

large works, the First and Second Symphonies, the psychology of the man, his method of composing, may be discerned.
The E minor Symphony (stupidly thought by many
musicians to have points of style in common with Tchaikovsky, presumably on the strength of the fact that
Tchaikovsky also wrote a symphony in E minor – and so did
Brahms, for that matter), could have been written by one man
only and that man Sibelius. After the statement of the big
tune of the Allegro Energico there is an abrupt transition to
a pianissimo of tremolo strings; then we hear the authentic
voice, flutes in thirds, followed by a wail of wood-wind; and
next comes a pulsation in the bass, insistent and strenuous
and uneven in accent, with the weaker instruments
struggling for articulation, empty lungs of effort. From the
Sibelius of this passage to the Sibelius of the Fifth Symphony is a progress or linked-chain of development as
natural as that which binds the Brahms of the F sharp minor
Piano Sonata to the Brahms of the Fourth Symphony. The
fashionable intelligences must face the fact that in Sibelius
the young barbarian was the father of the man; that they
harboured in their midst an untamed force who did not
change his nature simply because with the passing of time
he dispensed with lusty speech and preferred the subtlety of
implication.

Sibelius lived to see himself 'taken up' by well-bred
worthies who, I fear, may have suffered disconcerting moments when, as they got to know him better, he committed
acts of atavism from time to time and forgot his manners,
and also forgot where he extraordinarily and captivatingly
(as Henry James would phrase it) happened to be.

III

In the First and Second Symphonies Sibelius shakes traditional form to its foundations; not since Beethoven's hammer-blows and double-bass rumblings (in the Ninth) has any symphony suffered disturbances as vast as the seismic upheavals of Sibelius in E minor which come after the convulsions of the fugato in the development section of the andante, for example; also that incredible tuba passage in the slow movement of the Second Symphony, where the instrument sprawls and emits awakening breath and heaves itself from the encompassing and baleful gloom of the orchestra like some monster emerging from the primordial slime. But there is no vain show of energy in these gigantic stretchings of the limbs of the young giant Sibelius; his violence never runs to the hysteria of Tchaikovsky's reiterations of brass and his panic-stricken stampedes of sequences. The storms and turbulence of Sibelius are controlled; there is in every cyclone of nature a calm pivotal spot around which the fury revolves, giving strength to wildness. So with Sibelius; even in the period of his Sturm und Drang, when he let himself go without regard for his buttons, free, varied, humane, familiar, extravagant and never parsimonious, as in his later music he is often inclined to be.

In the First and Second Symphonies, Sibelius glories in excess, in deep quaffings from the pint-pot of life. He justified the austerity of his old age by saying that while other composers gave cocktails to the world he offered us cold water. For my part, I must confess to some slight amusement at the idea of Sibelius as an authority on cold water for the purposes of liquid refreshment to be taken internally. The reformed rake, of course, insists on an extreme of austerity to which the natural-born puritan would never subscribe; abstinence becomes for him a positive not a negative virtue, a case of perpetual watchfulness, with constant 'Get thee behind me's'. In one or two of the works of what may be called Sibelius's Third or Aqueous Period, we can catch the composer out as he glances thirstily towards the old wine-bin. At the very end of the Seventh Symphony, there comes a sudden splash of colour from the *Valse Triste*, one of the most atavistic passages in music. There are moments when my admiration of the matured genius of Sibelius is troubled by a question not easily answered – need the reformation have gone so far? Why so much water, many times iced below zero? 'I shall refine myself no finer than I am', said Sir Toby Belch. Can we truly and honestly get the Third Symphony and the Sixth into the Sibelian canon, for here are two compositions as inhibited and anaemic as any I know? As an artist grows older he naturally simplifies and subtilizes his expression, concentrates it and tires of purple patches and the old conceits; the development of all geniuses is from profuseness to reticence and thorough relevance. The crutches of explanatory clauses are laid aside; instinct has acquired a logic that moves swifter than that of the intellect. Admitting and knowing these things the doubt remains whether Sibelius has not here and there made a luxury of abstinence. Beethoven in his late quartets cut out all unnecessary formalism; he composed by ellipsis, so to say; he turned his vision inwards and frequently seemed to forget that though he himself was deaf, music herself is not likewise deaf. Still, even Beethoven did not, in his most austere period, deny his art a long flowing and free melody and a share of sensuous decoration – the slow movement of the F major Quartet, Op. 135 obviously is musical and addressed in the first place to the sensuous ear.

At this point, the reader may be girding his loins preparatory to falling on me for committing the worst impertinence of criticism, which is to object to a genius for being what he is, and not otherwise; and also because apparently I am presuming to argue that Sibelius would have been a greater artist if he had developed as I should have wished, and not as he himself, or his genius, decreed. Let me hasten with an assurance – I am aware that each genius creates the laws and standards by which criticism must measure him. The object must be seen and considered as it really is and estimated with reference only to its own power. It is by keeping my eye on Sibelius himself that I am persuaded to believe that his works suffer contradictions which cannot be explained in terms of the inevitable fluctuations in an artist's work, from his best to his not quite so good. Every man of genius has his lapses. I do not trouble about the banalities of Sibelius; as I have shown, they sprang from a certain and not essential cause. I am discussing now a change of method, even of musical aesthetic, which brought about inhibitions and reticences with an abruptness so stark that it is extremely difficult to discover the via media, the natural bridge, from the Second Symphony and its great range and musical power, to the thin-spun Third, where Sibelius comes out in all his strength only intermittently, as though by stealth. The monotony of the Sixth Symphony, a pale monotony of reiterated notes and rhythms, actually suggests that Sibelius has turned from cold water to lemonade; the Sixth Symphony lacks the edge of cold water. The First, Second and Fifth Symphonies are, for all their naturalism and disdain of the human scene, invigorating. The Third and Sixth Symphonies cover much the same ground; but naturalism and animism have been expelled, and in their place we have a mild echo of folk-music – mere regionalism, instead of the timeless landscape and the void beyond. The Fourth Symphony is like a spare unworked quarry of music; it is unique, no doubt – a

symphony of shadows; sometimes we cannot see the shape
of it; the pulse is low for the most part; the blood is cold.
I cannot agree to call the Fourth Symphony tragic. Tragedy
is stimulating; the effect generally achieved by Sibelius in
A minor is depression. The Sibelian formulae have frozen
in the night.

When we turn to the Fifth Symphony we shall find
support for my presumption – that the true Sibelius is, as
might have been expected, the original Sibelius of the
Second Symphony grown older; the sap of youth generates
here the stronger and more experienced tree. Long-
lengthed tunes do not occur in the Fifth Symphony maybe,
but the juice and cadence of great melody are present, in
every stem and branch of a masterpiece which in turn sums
up all the composer's aspects as man and as artist. First, we
find in this work a natural and unlaboured transition to
that process of closer integration which we must expect
from genius as it attains mastery. The energy and variety of
the spendthrift Sibelius are properly conserved in the Fifth
Symphony; ripeness for a while falls over the landscape;
the pizzicato andante is the one example I can find in
Sibelius of humane charm and tenderness; it is an intermezzo full of delicious and surprising turns of phrase and
rhythm. All that is original and lasting in Sibelius is, I
think, contained in the Fifth Symphony. The touch is
certain from the beginning. A horn call lures us at once
into the circle; Sibelius has a rare sense of the association-
value of a cadence. With a consummate hand he gathers
together all the essential strands and textures of his art so
far woven by him; and economy does not lead to parsimony.
Power and richness emerge now. As soon as we are drawn
into the first movement, the mists float as usual, and the
echoes of legends awake; then the familiar thirds of the
wood-wind run ahead; the will-o'-the-wisps flicker as

Sibelius uses the points of his fiddlers' bows to produce natural harmonies. A swaying figure in the bass, mysterious and processional, half enchants and half afrights the ear; we are bound to follow, whether to the heart's gladness or to the charnel house. The mists thicken; we are losing ourselves. A pitiful wailing in the bassoons, marked *lugubre* and *patetico* chills the marrow, until the brass announces the call we heard at the outset of our adventures; it is a note of confidence and self-reliance. A solo trumpet calls the movement home, and it obeys in a gathering race, *vivace molto*, the instruments seeming to tumble over one another before Sibelius brusquely ends the clamour as though with the stroke of an axe.

After the intermezzo, the symphony returns again to the eternal landscape. The strings race along as usual, leaves on the wind, the texture again thickening imperceptibly. Another swaying pendulum tune is heard, first on the 'cellos and basses, then on the horns. This is the movement's main theme and the symphony's catharsis and *deus ex machina* rolled into one. I cannot explain the magic of this simple theme. Sibelius does not linger with it; the strings resume their journey, seeking something, nobody knows what. The tempo broadens; here comes the crown of the work, and one of the noblest moments in the music of our time. The trumpets intone the swaying theme, solemn now, and it is followed twice by a descending four-note figure on the violins: simply that and nothing more, yet changed by genius to sounds that make the mind proud and swell the heart and soften it at the same time. The climax is splendidly dissonant; gold and brass. There is a growing arch; then with six peremptory chords, long-spaced and not easy to time, Sibelius dismisses us. 'There', he seems to say. 'Take it or leave it. That is my faith; that is my music.'

IV

Genius and originality in the arts depend on a capacity to feel life or nature, or some aspect of life or nature, and to convey this feeling in fresh and vital images or arrangements of sound, line and colour, with an intensity that enriches and renews the materials of expression. The original creator draws through his temperament the stuff of his medium and likewise his hand becomes subdued 'to that it works in'. By virtue of the range of the artist's feelings and of the range of his ideas and expression will the order and quality of his genius be established. Grieg obviously is not as great as Beethoven, though Grieg fully realizes in music all that is in him, and feels as strongly as his nature will allow, an aspect of life; and he sets it down in delightful arrangements of his art. Beethoven stands higher than Grieg because his capacity to feel is wider and deeper, with a proportionately wider and deeper command over the materials of his art.

Sibelius changed the face and colour of music. He found his right tone – a tone unheard until he drew the elements of orchestral sound through his temperament. He has expressed powerfully one aspect of nature; nature sublimely indifferent to the tragi-comedy of men and women; nature as tragi-comedy in and by herself. The question to be answered is whether he did not consider too closely this single aspect and failed to achieve that universality which is the usual mark of the highest order of genius. That he set to music the landscape of his country we have seen; but as Dr Johnson said, one green field is very much like another; certainly the substance and atmosphere and informing spirit of certain of the compositions of Sibelius are much alike. Do we discover a different world, an essentially differently imagined art, as we pass from *En Saga* to

Night Ride and Sunrise; from the Fourth Symphony to *Tapiola*? The method becomes more subtle as we modulate to the more mature artist; but does the conception alter at bottom, does the music not exhibit much the same processes, and proceed according to much the same formula? If we were somehow to lose the scores of the Third and Sixth Symphonies, *Tapiola* and *Night Ride and Sunrise*, would gaps in our knowledge of the style and psychology of the composer loom importantly, so long as we could preserve the Second and Fifth Symphonies, the Violin Concerto, the beautiful *Swan of Tuonela*, and the Seventh Symphony? These works present Sibelius in the round; but even here we do not find a music for Everyman; Sibelius, though original and powerful, works in a single track. I have sometimes thought that he is a composer for the unmusical countries of the earth; I cannot imagine many of his works listened to under the blue sky of Italy; or in the places where art is a warmth, a grace, as well as an expression. Like most original geniuses, Sibelius has been poorly served by his cult; they have cried him up as one of the giants of music. The truth, as the future may see it, is that he has written an amount of music not related to any other in style or conception; music with a power which alternately smoulders and burns in a forge well removed from the main thoroughfare. It is not conceivable that any work of Sibelius will enter the minds of men and women the world over, as the masterpieces of Bach, Beethoven, Mozart have done, or as the less imposing masterpieces of Tchaikovsky have done. I should hesitate, personally, to rank Sibelius higher than Tchaikovsky in point of sheer genius – if it comes to that. Comparisons are 'odorous' maybe; still they need to be made if only to save a great artist from his friends – or his cult.

There is a school of criticism which esteems Sibelius mostly for his contributions to symphonic form. Ernest

Newman has written that the logical end of the symphony is one-movement form – a single movement in which the old formal structure would be dispensed with, stereotyped balance of sections, keys, subjects and so on. In this one-movement symphony, form would be simply the correlative of the ideas, 'and therefore in the final result not a "form" at all, but simply *form*, a way of setting about things and getting to the desired end that would hold good only of the particular ideas of the particular work'. Mr Newman demonstrates how *Tapiola* is constructed mainly out of one theme, 'the evolutions of which correspond so unerringly to the evolutions of the poetic idea that it is impossible to say either that the vicissitudes of the music come from the changing pictures in the composer's mind or that the variations in the music have themselves suggested new phases of the central poetic vision'. The same unifying procedure, Mr Newman claims, controls the single movement of the Seventh Symphony of Sibelius, in which he declares there are no sections corresponding *'even remotely'* (my italics) to the definite divisions of the older symphony. Now laying aside for the moment the question whether the content of *Tapiola* and the Seventh Symphony is vital and interesting enough to keep any sort of form alive – and Mr Newman occasionally seems more interested in architecture than in whether the building is worth entering – I hasten emphatically to deny that in the Seventh Symphony there are no sections corresponding 'even remotely' to the definite divisions of the older symphony. Four movements may clearly be discerned in Sibelius' Number Seven: first *a slow adagio* ending with the repetition of the ascending scale-passage that begins the work; then we have a bridge-passage, with palpable sequences for oboes and clarinets; this transition changes to six-four time, and now the symphony goes into its scherzo, which broadens to an allegro with the accented notes of the one unmistakably lyrical melody of the work. The fourth movement is heralded by strenuous imitative figures which recall the race into the finale of the Second Symphony; there is the familiar Sibelian heave and gathering of energy for a final throw, then the movement – the fourth movement – is hoisted like a coping stone, to crown the end. The telescoping of these divisions is skilfully done, with subtle interchange of material; none the less the symphony has its classical ground-plan. I do not understand why such a spatch-cocking of parts should be received by competent authorities as obviously an advance in symphonic logic; it compresses no doubt, but does it really lead to a new way of symphonic thinking? The point for serious critical attention is the quality of the wine – or the water – not the shape of the bottle. I find the beginning and the end of the Seventh Symphony noble enough; the middle sections strike me as either trivial or unrealized. The work might have thrived on expansion; after all, is not a tabloid symphony a con-tradiction in terms? Is not the very essence of the symphonic style gradual enlargement, a unity achieved not by omission but by synthesis; a harvest and not a fast? In the Fifth Symphony Sibelius does not lose sight of the classical symphony pattern. The highly individual string quartet is in the sonata-fantasia style, with a freedom and discursive-ness of argument and mood not unlike, certainly, the late quartets of Beethoven.

But it is as irrelevant to discuss the rude imperious Sibelius in terms of form and the new logic as it would be to analyse the chantings of some ancient bard in terms of iambics, hexameters, inverted stresses and what-not. One of Sibelius's compositions is called *En Saga*; the whole of his work could support the same simple description, with all its associations of remote poetry, of grandeur and independence

of gesture and utterance, a song and story not of the present
or of the past, but one as timeless as tradition. Sibelius sits
alone in the house of music rather away from the hearth
and the logs and the company; he says little, and sometimes
by taciturnity alone he makes an impression of deep thinking. He is simple yet subtle, like all who keep apart; as he
sits he drinks and meditates. *Is* it always cold water now? –
once on a time it was occasionally something stronger and
headier.